IRAN NUCLEAR DEAL OVERSIGHT: IMPLEMENTATION AND ITS CONSEQUENCES

HEARING

BEFORE THE

COMMITTEE ON FOREIGN AFFAIRS
HOUSE OF REPRESENTATIVES

ONE HUNDRED FOURTEENTH CONGRESS

SECOND SESSION

FEBRUARY 11, 2016

Serial No. 114–143

Printed for the use of the Committee on Foreign Affairs

Available via the World Wide Web: http://www.foreignaffairs.house.gov/ or
http://www.gpo.gov/fdsys/

U.S. GOVERNMENT PUBLISHING OFFICE

98–602PDF   WASHINGTON : 2016

For sale by the Superintendent of Documents, U.S. Government Publishing Office
Internet: bookstore.gpo.gov   Phone: toll free (866) 512–1800; DC area (202) 512–1800
Fax: (202) 512–2104   Mail: Stop IDCC, Washington, DC 20402–0001

(II)

CONTENTS

IRAN NUCLEAR DEAL OVERSIGHT: IMPLEMENTATION AND ITS CONSEQUENCES

THURSDAY, FEBRUARY 11, 2016

House of Representatives,
Committee on Foreign Affairs,
Washington, DC.

The committee met, pursuant to notice, at 10:04 a.m., in room 2172 Rayburn House Office Building, Hon. Edward Royce (chairman of the committee) presiding.

Chairman ROYCE. This hearing will come to order. This morning the committee continues our extensive oversight of the Obama administration's nuclear agreement with Iran, and its consequences for the national security of the United States, the consequences also for our allies. As you may know here, I feel those consequences are quite dire.

January 16th was "Implementation Day," and that marked an historic turning point in the Middle East because in a snap, Iran's record was cleared, its pariah status was dropped, and this reconnected Iran to the international trade and financial system. Now, with access to $100 billion in unfrozen assets and sanctions wiped away, Iran has instantly become the dominant country in the region. The regime has achieved this all without having to end its aggression against its neighbors. It still calls for the overthrow of the governments in Bahrain and in Saudi Arabia and in other regional states. It has done it without swearing off on its support for terrorism.

And the Iranian economy was, frankly, prior to this hemorrhaging—hemorrhaging because the sanctions which we had pushed had worked. The sanctions we pushed in 2010 and 2012 had led by 2013 to the implosion of the economy there. Now, now Iran's leaders are predicting swift growth. And they are probably right, because we see these European countries that have observed that the sanctions dam is broken, and they are sprinting into the Iranian market to cut billions in deals and to invest there, and they are making a mockery of the administration's claim that sanctions could "snap back" if Iran cheats. You tell me if these companies are going to turn back when Iran stiffs international inspectors.

The Revolutionary Guards, already Iran's "most powerful economic actor"—now those are the words of our Treasury Department—the "most powerful economic actor," why would that be the Iranian Guard? Because they are the ones that nationalized the construction firms and the companies. So they are only going to grow more powerful with this additional international investment.

Just hours after the agreement's implementation, the regime disqualified 2,967 of roughly 3,000 moderate candidates from running in the parliamentary elections later this month. And after the administration finally responded to Iran's missile tests with very minor sanctions, very de minimis sanctions, Iran's ''moderate'' President, as he is called, ordered the military to accelerate its intercontinental ballistic missile program. That is aimed here—at the United States—and it is designed to carry a nuclear payload. That ICBM program that they are running where the Ayatollah says it is every military's mission to help mass produce, and duty to help mass produce, ICBMs.

Now worse, the administration continues to go out of its way to appease the Iranian regime, and even thanked Iran after it recently seized 10 U.S. sailors in a highly provocative act, if you ask me. I mean when was the last time we have seen U.S. sailors taken off their ship with their hands behind their heads, guns trained on them, their ships stripped, photographs for propaganda purposes taken, photographs of one of these sailors crying appearing in the Iranian press, and then medals, medals given to those Iranian agents who took them into custody.

It appears the administration is determined to protect this deal at all costs. And just look at how the Obama administration backed away from a new bipartisan U.S. law ending visa waiver travel for those who travel to Iran, Iraq, Syria, after an outcry, after an outcry from the Iranian regime. And the administration has now decided to basically ignore the laws—and Iran's ongoing sponsorship of terrorism—by stretching a narrow national security waiver far beyond reason. President Obama signed this bill into law, but has essentially allowed Iran's Supreme Leader to veto it.

And in an unusual move, the State Department settled a decades-old financial settlement the day after ''implementation day,'' sending the Iranian regime a check for $1.7 billion. As you know, Mr. Ambassador, the committee eagerly awaits answers from the State Department to the many questions surrounding that surprise payment. The administration had countless opportunities to seek committee input to this matter in advance, but purposefully did not do so. That's the conclusion I have to reach.

Iran has never complied with any, any of its past nuclear-related agreements. We are watching this to see if this time it will be different. But even if Iran meets all the administration's expectations, in a few short years the accord will leave it the dominant power in the Middle East, and only steps away from the capability to produce nuclear weapons on an industrial scale. All the while—and this is the most vexing part to me—all the while, Iran's leaders continued on Friday to chant ''Death to America.'' Many of us are struggling to see how this tilt toward Iran makes us safer.

I now recognize the ranking member for any opening comments he may have.

Mr. ENGEL. Thank you, Mr. Chairman. And thank you again for calling this hearing.

Ambassador Mull, welcome to the Foreign Affairs Committee, Mr. Smith. I know, Ambassador, your current role is the latest stop on a distinguished career as an American diplomat. And no matter whether we supported the Iran deal or opposed it, we are fortunate to have you as our point person on implementation and we are grateful for your service.

Mr. Smith, welcome to you. Thank you for your service. Your office has led the way in cracking down on some of Iran's worst offenses. In my view, Treasury could be doing even more if we had an Undersecretary for Terrorism and Financial Intelligence. But the nomination of Adam Szubin is bogged down in the Senate Banking Committee, despite the urgent need to cut off Iran, ISIS, North Korea, and others from their resources. The Senate should confirm Mr. Szubin immediately.

This is far from the first time the Foreign Affairs Committee has held a hearing on Iran. We have held many hearings. We understand exactly what the deal was and is. But today's hearing is distinctly different from any we have had before because the Iran deal has been implemented, nuclear-related sanctions have been lifted, and Iran no longer has enough fuel to make a nuclear weapon.

Again, no matter what anyone's position was on the Iran deal—and I strongly opposed the Iran deal—this ship has left port, and now we need to decide which course to chart. One option would be to continue bringing up legislation designed to undermine the deal. The House has passed two bills like this already, largely along party lines. These are symbolic votes, none that have become law. In my view, they are not a valuable use of this committee or Congress' time.

So I don't think we should treat the Iran deal the way we have dealt with the Affordable Care Act, voting again and again to repeal it even though it is a settled issue.

Again, I didn't like it. I voted against it but it passed. So there is another option. And the other option, the one I support, is to work in a bipartisan manner to hold Iran's feet to the fire and ensure there are serious consequences with nefarious behavior. There is a lot we can and should be doing, and I am confident that we can work across the aisle to find common ground that we can build on.

Iran remains the world's most active state sponsor of terror and a chronic human rights abuser. Iran continues to break into national law with impunity. We don't trust Iran, and our policies must reflect that. That is why I am glad we slapped new sanctions on Iran for testing two medium range ballistic missiles late last year, tests that were a blatant violation of the U.N. Security Council Resolution governing the nuclear deal.

And there are other problems we need to address. An Iran freed from most sanctions can spread more resources to bad actors throughout the region, strengthening the murderous Assad regime, reinforcing Hezbollah, boosting the Houthis in Yemen, and supporting Shia militias in Iraq. As the chairman pointed out, it really is galling when after we sign an agreement with Iran, they continue, their leaders continue, to yell ''Death to America.'' It really is galling.

But we need to work together on new legislation that will crack down on this other dangerous behavior of Iran and shore up our allies and partners in the region. So, Ambassador Mull and Mr.

Smith, I look forward to hearing from you about the implementation of the JCPOA, the monitoring and verification that Iran is living up to its commitments, and what else we can be doing with respect to Iran, outside the scope of the nuclear deal, to help make our country safer and enhance stability in the region.

Iran had sanctions lifted because of the nuclear agreement. But there are a lot of things that Iran has not yet done, and there are a lot of bad things that Iran is doing that I think will warrant additional sanctions, for instance, Iran's continued support for terrorism. That is not something we can turn a blind eye to, and we shouldn't.

So we need to figure out the way we can be most effective, what we can do in respect to Iran, again outside the scope of the nuclear deal, because during the nuclear deal we were told, well, we can't really talk about anything else, we can only talk about the nuclear deal. And so, again, it is galling when we look at Iran.

It is, I think the frustration that you heard from the chairman is, frankly, the frustration that all of us have with Iran, Iranians and with their bad behavior and with their not changing at all after they sign an agreement, showing no good faith whatsoever, poking us in the eye, continuing to walk on the line and walk over on their own way. We really must hold their feet to the fire.

So I look forward to your testimony, gentlemen.

Thank you, Mr. Chairman. I yield back.

Chairman ROYCE. Thank you, Mr. Engel.

So this morning we are joined by a very distinguished panel. We have Ambassador Mull, who serves as the Lead Coordinator for Iran Nuclear Implementation at the Department of State. Prior to this appointment, Ambassador Mull served as the Ambassador to Poland and as Executive Secretary of the State Department.

Mr. Smith is the Acting Director of the Office of Foreign Assets Control at the Treasury Department. Prior to joining OFAC, Mr. Smith served as an expert at the United Nations al-Qaeda and Taliban Sanctions Committee and as a trial attorney at the U.S. Department of Justice.

Without objection, the witnesses' full prepared statements will be made part of the record. And members here will have 5 calendar days to submit any statements or questions or extraneous material for the record.

So, if you would, Mr. Ambassador, please summarize your remarks. We will go to you first.

STATEMENT OF THE HONORABLE STEPHEN D. MULL, LEAD COORDINATOR FOR IRAN NUCLEAR IMPLEMENTATION, U.S. DEPARTMENT OF STATE

Ambassador MULL. It is a pleasure, Chairman Royce, Ranking Member Engel, and all the distinguished members of this panel. I appreciate the opportunity to meet with you today to testify on the progress we have had on implementing the Joint Comprehensive Plan of Action, or the JCPOA.

This is a really important deal for America's security, and that of our friends and allies around the world. And I welcome Congress' oversight and partnership in making sure we get this exactly right.

On January 16th, the International Atomic Energy Agency issued a report verifying that Iran had completed its key nuclear steps under the JCPOA, thus reaching Implementation Day. Those commitments signified that Iran had dismantled two-thirds of its installed centrifuge capacity, including all of its most advanced centrifuge machines, and drastically rolled back its enrichment program, which had been growing exponentially over the past decade.

It shipped out almost all, about 25,000 pounds worth, of its enriched uranium material. Going forward, Iran can possess no more than 300 kilograms of up to 3.67 percent enriched uranium for the next 15 years.

Further, Iran removed the core of its Arak reactor and rendered it inoperable by filling it with concrete, cutting off the path by which Iran could have produced significant amounts of weapons grade plutonium.

Iran placed its nuclear program under an unprecedented and continuous IAEA verification and monitoring regime, using modern technologies like electronic seals and online enrichment monitors that can detect and report cheating. The IAEA also has oversight of Iran's entire nuclear fuel cycle, from uranium mills to enrichment facilities and centrifuge production plants, ensuring that Iran cannot divert nuclear materials to a potential covert program without detection.

Furthermore, any goods and technology usable for nuclear purposes must now go through a procurement channel administered by the United Nations Security Council, creating yet another layer of transparency, oversight, and monitoring into Iran's nuclear program.

Iran is now also provisionally applying, as a result of this agreement, the Additional Protocol to its Comprehensive Safeguards Agreement with the IAEA. This, along with the JCPOA's special provisions to address disputes regarding IAEA access to an undeclared location within a short period of time, ensures that the IAEA will have all the access it needs to keep ongoingly verify Iran's commitments.

As a result of these actions, in keeping with the deal, on January 16th the United States, the European Union, and the United Nations Security Council lifted nuclear-related sanctions against Iran, allowing the resumption of some international commercial and investment activity with Iran. In keeping with our commitments, we will not try to block commercial activity that the JCPOA permits. However, we will be closely monitoring it to be ready to act with the substantial existing authorities that we still have as a government if that activity supports goals that are hostile to our interests in Iran's terrorism or in Iran's ballistic missile program.

All U.S. sanctions on Iran that are not nuclear-related remain in effect. As evidenced just a few weeks ago when we designated for sanctions a number of individuals and entities for supporting Iran's ballistic missile program, the JCPOA in no way limits our ability, or will, to use these tools to respond to Iran's other destabilizing activities.

That is precisely why our allies and nations around the world support this deal: It eliminates the threat of a nuclear-armed Iran, it gives the international community unprecedented tools to ensure

Iran's nuclear program remains exclusively peaceful going forward, and it does not limit our ability to respond to Iran's destabilizing policies and actions. In sort, it makes the world safer for all of us.

Just a few weeks ago, Israeli Defense Forces Chief of Staff Lieutenant General Gadi Eisenkot acknowledged that the JCPOA reduces the immediate Iranian threat to Israel because it ''rolls back Iran's nuclear capability and deepens the monitoring capabilities'' of the international community into Tehran's activities. In those same remarks, Eisenkot also said that he believes that ''Iran will make great efforts to fulfill their side of the bargain.''

The JCPOA was not built on a prediction of what the future will bring. It is built on a solid verification regime. And my team and I will continue working every day to confirm that Iran is living up to its JCPOA commitments or face the consequences.

The administration looks forward to continuing to engage with this committee and with the Congress in general on this important topic. I look forward to answering your questions today.

Thank you.

[The prepared statement of Ambassador Mull follows:]

U.S. DEPARTMENT OF STATE

TESTIMONY OF:

AMBASSADOR STEPHEN D. MULL
LEAD COORDINATOR FOR IRAN NUCLEAR IMPLEMENTATION
DEPARTMENT OF STATE

BEFORE THE

UNITED STATES HOUSE OF REPRESENTATIVES
COMMITTEE ON FOREIGN AFFAIRS

ON

"IRAN NUCLEAR DEAL OVERSIGHT: IMPLEMENTATION AND ITS
CONSEQUENCES "

FEBRUARY 11, 2016
10:00 A.M.

2172 RAYBURN HOUSE OFFICE BUILDING
WASHINGTON, D.C.

Chairman Royce, Ranking Member Engel, distinguished Members of the Committee – I appreciate the opportunity to testify before you today on progress implementing the Joint Comprehensive Plan of Action, or JCPOA.

My name is Ambassador Steve Mull, and I am a 33 year veteran of the Foreign Service. Shortly after the JCPOA was concluded, Secretary Kerry asked me to return to Washington from my last post as U.S. Ambassador to Poland to serve as Lead Coordinator for implementing the JCPOA. In this job, I lead an interagency team composed of experts from within the Department of State, as well as at the Departments of Energy, the Treasury, and Commerce, among others, dedicated to this important work.

My job is focused on making sure the JCPOA achieves its one, crucial objective – an objective I know we all share – ensuring Iran's nuclear program is and remains exclusively peaceful. And I am pleased to report that we have made great progress toward that objective over the past six months, as Iran implemented all of its key nuclear-related commitments necessary to reach Implementation Day.

On January 16, the International Atomic Energy Agency issued a report verifying that Iran had completed its key nuclear steps under the JCPOA, thus reaching Implementation Day.

To reach Implementation Day, Iran had to verifiably complete key nuclear steps that substantially rolled back its nuclear program, placed its nuclear program under a comprehensive IAEA monitoring and verification regime, cut off all of its pathways to weapons-grade nuclear material, and lengthened its "breakout time" for enough fissile material for a single nuclear weapon from 2 to 3 months before the JCPOA to at least a year at present – if Iran were to change course, abandon the JCPOA and spring toward a bomb.. Let me highlight some examples.

In keeping with its commitments under the JCPOA, Iran has dismantled two-thirds of its installed centrifuge capacity including all of its most advanced centrifuge machines. Before the JCPOA, Iran had over 19,000 centrifuges. Today, it has just 6,104 of only its most primitive, first-generation centrifuges. And of those 6,104 machines, only 5,060 of them can be used to enrich uranium for the next decade.

Iran shipped out almost all of its enriched uranium stockpile. Pre-JCPOA, Iran had approximately 12,000 kilograms of enriched uranium. Now, Iran can have no more than 300 kilograms of up to 3.67% enriched uranium for the next 15 years. This, combined with Iran's dismantlement of two-thirds of its centrifuges, has effectively cut off Iran's uranium pathway to a nuclear weapon.

Iran removed the core of its Arak reactor and rendered it inoperable by filling it with concrete. This cut off the path by which Iran could have produced significant amounts of weapons grade plutonium. Now, the Arak reactor will be redesigned, in cooperation with a working group established under the JCPOA, ensuring that the reactor is used solely for peaceful purposes going forward.

Iran placed its nuclear program under an unprecedented IAEA verification and monitoring regime. Its key declared nuclear facilities are now under continuous monitoring using modern technologies like electronic seals and online enrichment monitors that can detect and report cheating. The IAEA also has oversight of Iran's entire nuclear fuel cycle, from uranium mills to enrichment facilities and centrifuge production plants, ensuring that Iran cannot divert nuclear materials to a potential covert program without detection.

Furthermore, any goods and technology potentially usable for nuclear purposes must now go through a procurement channel administered by the United Nations Security Council, creating yet another layer of transparency and monitoring into Iran's nuclear program.

Iran is now also provisionally applying the Additional Protocol to its Comprehensive Safeguards Agreement with the IAEA. This, along with the JCPOA's special provision to address disputes regarding IAEA access to an undeclared location within a short period of time, ensures that the IAEA will have the access it needs to verify Iran's commitments.

And finally, Iran has committed not to engage in activities, including at the research and development level, which could potentially contribute to the development of a nuclear explosive device.

These are just some of many steps Iran had to take to substantially roll back its nuclear program and reassure the world of the exclusively peaceful nature of the program before reaching Implementation Day. And just as Iran had commitments to meet, so too did the United States and our P5+1 and European Union partners.

On January 16, the United States and EU lifted nuclear-related sanctions against Iran. As a result of these actions, there are now more opportunities for legitimate business in Iran that is consistent with the JCPOA, and international banks and companies are beginning to explore those opportunities. As they proceed, it will be important that they have a clear understanding of the changed regulatory and sanctions environment with respect to Iran, and we are working closely with our colleagues at the Department of the Treasury to engage the international business community to answer their questions about the sanctions that have been lifted as well as those that remain in place.

But I want to emphasize, however, that this relief of nuclear-related sanctions is predicated on Iran's continued compliance with its commitments under the JCPOA. If Iran cheats or fails to meet its end of the bargain, the United States has an array of means to respond, including the ability to re-impose sanctions unilaterally, in part or in full, at any time.

As you know, our government both engages with Iran on its nuclear program and works with partners around the world to oppose Iran's actions on a host of issues unrelated to this nuclear deal. For example, we continue to have concerns and take actions to counter Iran's support for terrorism, its human rights abuses, and threats from its ballistic missile program. All U.S. sanctions on Iran that are not nuclear-related remain in effect. As evidenced just a few weeks ago when we designated for sanctions a number of individuals and entities for supporting Iran's ballistic missile program, the JCPOA in no way limits our ability or will to use these tools to respond to Iran's other destabilizing activities.

This is precisely why our allies and nations around the world support this deal – it eliminates the threat of a nuclear-armed Iran, gives the international community unprecedented tools to ensure Iran's nuclear program remains exclusively peaceful moving forward, and does not limit our ability to respond to Iran's destabilizing policies and actions. In short, it makes the world safer.

The JCPOA has received broad international support, including from our allies in the Gulf Cooperation Council (GCC) and over 100 countries around the world. It has been endorsed by the United Nations Security Council and multinational organizations such as the North Atlantic Treaty Organization.

And we have recently seen signs that Israel, our close partner and friend with whom we have had extensive consultations and more than a few disagreements over the JCPOA, is now publicly acknowledging the positive benefits of the JCPOA.

Speaking at an annual security conference in Tel Aviv a few weeks ago, Israel Defense Forces Chief of Staff Lieutenant General Gadi Eisenkot acknowledged that the JCPOA reduces the immediate Iranian threat to Israel because it "rolls back Iran's nuclear capability and deepens the monitoring capabilities" of the international community into Tehran's activities. In those same remarks, Eisenkot also said that he believes that, "Iran will make great efforts to fulfill their side of the bargain."

Of course, we will remain vigilant regarding Iran's compliance with the JCPOA. The JCPOA was not built on a prediction of what the future will bring. It was built on verification instead of trust, and my team and I will continue working every day to confirm that Iran is living up to its JCPOA commitments.

The Administration looks forward to continuing to engage with this Committee and with Congress more broadly on this important topic. I look forward to answering your questions today.

###

Chairman ROYCE. Thank you, Ambassador.
Mr. SMITH.

STATEMENT OF MR. JOHN SMITH, ACTING DIRECTOR, OFFICE OF FOREIGN ASSETS CONTROL, U.S. DEPARTMENT OF THE TREASURY

Mr. SMITH. Good morning, Chairman Royce, Ranking Member Engel, and distinguished members of the committee. Thank you for the invitation to appear today before you to discuss our actions on Implementation Day of the Joint Comprehensive Plan of Action, or the JCPOA, and our efforts to enhance and enforce our Iran-related sanctions going forward.

I will be addressing the key steps that my office, the Treasury Department's Office of Foreign Assets Control, or OFAC, took to fulfill the U.S. Government's sanctions-related commitments on Implementation Day. And I will address the many Iran-related sanctions authorities that remain in place and how we approach our responsibilities to enforce those authorities.

The JCPOA is a strong deal that protects the national security of the United States and our partners and allies overseas. And Implementation Day was a significant milestone of the JCPOA. In exchange for Iran verifiably completing its key nuclear-related commitments under the JCPOA, we lifted nuclear-related sanctions on Iran.

We took our steps on Implementation Day only after the International Atomic Energy Agency verified that Iran had completed its key nuclear commitments under the JCPOA. The deal gives us the necessary flexibility to respond to Iran if it fails to comply with its JCPOA commitments, including the ability to fully snap back international and domestic sanctions. As the agency tasked with implementing and enforcing U.S. economic sanctions, we are clear-eyed about the fact that Iran remains a state sponsor of terrorism and continues to engage in other destabilizing activities. We believe it is crucial to continue to implement and enforce the sanctions that remain in place.

On Implementation Day, the United States took action with respect to sanctions in two key areas. The first, and most significant, was to effectuate the lifting of nuclear-related secondary sanctions, which are sanctions that are directed toward non-U.S. persons for activity outside of U.S. jurisdiction.

The second area concerns three relatively narrow exceptions to our primary embargo on Iran, which remains in place. On Implementation Day, OFAC issued a Statement of Licensing Policy establishing a favorable licensing policy with respect to exports or re-exports to Iran of commercial passenger aircraft and related parts and services to be used exclusively for commercial passenger aviation. We also issued a general license authoring the importation into the United States of Iranian-origin carpets and foodstuffs, and we issued a general license authorizing U.S.-owned or -controlled foreign entities to engage in activities involving Iran that are consistent with the JCPOA and applicable U.S. laws and regulations.

To assist the public in understanding all the sanctions modifications effective on Implementation Day, OFAC also published on our Web site a summary of the actions we took, as well as hyperlinks to documents that explain in detail the contours of the sanctions lifting, including a guidance document that describes in detail the lifting of the nuclear-related sanctions and the sanctions that remain, a set of more than 85 frequently asked questions, and information on the changes that we made to the various sanctions lists.

While we have fulfilled our Implementation Day commitments to lift the sanctions specified in the JCPOA, OFAC continues to administer a robust sanctions regime targeting Iran outside of the nuclear arena, and the range of Iran's troubling activities. Broadly, the U.S. primary embargo on Iran remains in place. This means that U.S. persons generally remain prohibited from engaging in transactions or dealings with Iran or Iranian entities, unless such transactions are exempt from regulations or authorized by OFAC.

In addition, secondary sanctions continue to attach to the more than 200 Iran-related individuals and entities on OFAC's Specially Designated Nationals and Blocked Persons List, what we call our SDN List, as well as any such persons we add to the SDN List in the future. And Treasury remains fully committed to using our existing sanctions authorities to target Iran's support for terrorism, its human rights abuses, its ballistic missile program, and its destabilizing activities in the region.

Thank you. And I welcome your questions.

[The prepared statement of Mr. Smith follows:]

Testimony of John E. Smith,
Acting Director of the Office of Foreign Assets Control,
United States Department of the Treasury
on the Joint Comprehensive Plan of Action (JCPOA) Implementation Day
and Continuing Monitoring and Enforcement

United States House of Representatives Committee on Foreign Affairs
February 11, 2016

Good morning, Chairman Royce, Ranking Member Engel, and distinguished members of the committee. Thank you for the invitation to appear before you today to discuss our actions on Implementation Day of the Joint Comprehensive Plan of Action (JCPOA) and our efforts to enforce our Iran-related sanctions going forward.

I'll be addressing the key steps that my office, the Treasury Department's Office of Foreign Assets Control (OFAC), took to fulfill the U.S. Government's sanctions commitments on Implementation Day of the JCPOA. And I'll address the many Iran-related sanctions authorities that remain in place and how we approach our responsibility to enforce those authorities.

The JCPOA is a strong deal that protects the national security of the United States and our partners and allies overseas. And Implementation Day was a significant milestone of the JCPOA. In exchange for Iran verifiably completing its key nuclear-related commitments under the

JCPOA, which closed off all of its pathways to a nuclear weapon and put in place robust monitoring and transparency measures going forward, we lifted nuclear-related sanctions on Iran. The JCPOA, as others have said, is based on verification, not trust. In fact, we took our steps on Implementation Day only after the International Atomic Energy Agency verified that Iran had completed its key commitments. Furthermore, the deal gives us the necessary flexibility to respond to Iran if it fails to comply with its JCPOA commitments, including the ability to fully snap-back international and domestic sanctions. And as the agency tasked with implementing and enforcing U.S. economic sanctions, we are clear-eyed about the fact that Iran remains a State Sponsor of Terrorism and continues to engage in other destabilizing activities. We believe it is crucial to continue to implement and enforce the sanctions that remain.

On Implementation Day, the United States took actions with respect to sanctions in two key areas. The first, and most significant, was to effectuate the lifting of nuclear-related secondary sanctions, which are sanctions that are directed toward non-U.S. persons for activity wholly outside of U.S. jurisdiction. The sanctions that were lifted applied to Iran's banking, financial, insurance, energy, petrochemical, and automotive sectors; shipping and shipbuilding sectors and port operators; trade in gold and precious metals; trade in certain materials and software; and associated services for each of these categories. In addition, OFAC removed more than 400 individuals and entities from the Specially Designated Nationals and Blocked Persons List (the "SDN List"), meaning that secondary sanctions no longer attach to significant transactions with, or the provision of material support to, those individuals and entities.

The second area concerns three relatively narrow exceptions to our primary embargo on Iran. On Implementation Day, OFAC issued: (1) a Statement of Licensing Policy establishing a favorable licensing policy with respect to exports or re-exports to Iran of commercial passenger aircraft and related parts and services to be used exclusively for commercial passenger aviation; (2) a general license authorizing the importation into the United States of Iranian-origin carpets and foodstuffs, including pistachios and caviar; and (3) a general license authorizing U.S.-owned or -controlled foreign entities to engage in activities involving Iran that are consistent with the JCPOA and applicable U.S. laws and regulations.

To give effect to U.S. commitments with respect to sanctions on Implementation Day, the President issued an Executive Order that revoked four Iran sanctions-related Executive orders and sections of a fifth, a series of waiver determinations and findings with respect to relevant statutory sanctions issued by the State Department came into effect; and OFAC took the actions that I just outlined.

To assist the public in understanding all the sanctions modifications effective on Implementation Day, OFAC published on its website a summary of the actions taken, as well as hyperlinks to documents that explain in detail the contours of the sanctions lifting. These documents are: (1) a guidance document that describes in detail the lifting of nuclear-related sanctions under the JCPOA and the sanctions that remain; (2) a set of more than 85 frequently asked questions; (3) the texts of the Statement of Licensing Policy and two general licenses; and (4) information on the changes we made to the various sanctions lists administered by OFAC.

While we have fulfilled our Implementation Day commitments to lift the sanctions specified in the JCPOA, OFAC continues to administer a robust sanctions regime targeting Iran outside of the nuclear arena, and its troubling activities. Broadly, the U.S. primary embargo on Iran is still in place. This means that U.S. persons generally remain prohibited from engaging in transactions or dealings with Iran or Iranian entities, unless such activities are exempt from regulation or authorized by OFAC. Limited exceptions include longstanding general licenses that authorize U.S. persons to engage in certain activities involving Iran, such as the export of agricultural products, medicine, and medical supplies to Iran, as well as certain items to facilitate Iranian persons' access to communications and the Internet. U.S. persons must also continue to block the assets of the Government of Iran and Iranian financial institutions. Furthermore, we have retained sanctions authorities targeting Iran's support for terrorism, its human rights abuses, its ballistic missile program, and its destabilizing activities in the region. And, we will continue to exercise these authorities to counter Iran's behavior, as we did on January 17, when OFAC designated eleven individuals and entities in connection with their support to Iran's ballistic missile program.

In addition, secondary sanctions continue to attach to the more than 200 Iran-related individuals and entities that remain on the SDN List, as well as any such persons we add to the SDN List in the future. This means that non-U.S. persons who conduct significant transactions with, or provide material support to, designated parties may face being cut off from the U.S. financial system. Further even after Implementation Day, secondary sanctions continue to attach to significant financial transactions, including those by foreign financial institutions with Iran's Islamic Revolutionary Guards Corps, or any individual or entity sanctioned in connection with Iran's support for international terrorism or its ballistic missile program.

Finally, of the more than 400 individuals and entities that were taken off the SDN List on Implementation Day, roughly 200 of those were placed on a new OFAC list – the E.O. 13599 list – to indicate that they remain blocked persons under U.S. law. These individuals and entities are those OFAC has previously identified as the Government of Iran or Iranian financial institutions. While secondary sanctions no longer apply to most transactions involving individuals and entities on the E.O. 13599 list, U.S. persons continue to have an obligation to block property in which such persons have an interest and are prohibited generally from dealing with them.

In addition to the sanctions that we have in place to counter Iran's destabilizing activities, we also have avenues to swiftly respond if Iran stops complying with its commitments under the JCPOA. The JCPOA contains a dispute resolution mechanism whereby any JCPOA participant can refer any instances of alleged non-compliance to the Joint Commission, which provides a multilateral forum for addressing issues that arise. If we are unable to address these issues, the United States has the ability to quickly re-impose all of the national and multilateral sanctions that are lifted. At the UN, we have established a snapback mechanism that provides the unilateral ability to re-impose UN sanctions that were in place on Iran prior to Implementation Day without the worry of a veto by any member of the P-5. Finally, the United States has a range of options short of full snapback to respond to smaller breaches of the JCPOA, should we so choose.

As I said at the beginning of my testimony, the JCPOA is a strong deal that protects the national security of the United States and our partners and allies overseas. Iran has taken its nuclear-related steps, as verified by the International Atomic Energy Agency, and in turn, we have lifted nuclear-related sanctions pursuant to our commitments under the JCPOA. Treasury remains fully committed to using our existing sanctions authorities to address Iran's support for terrorism, its human rights abuses, its ballistic missile program, and its destabilizing activities in the region.

Thank you. I welcome your questions.

Chairman ROYCE. Thank you, Mr. Smith.

Let me start, Mr. Smith, with the fact that you note in your testimony that there are still hefty secondary sanctions available for anyone who is connected to the IRGC or Iran's support for terrorism. Why then haven't we been able to do more on Mahan Air, which is the Iranian passenger airline that also happens to be the favorite with the country's Islamic Revolutionary Guard Corps?

The IRGC uses this particular company to ferry its weapons and its personnel into Syria to aid the Syrian regime. And after Quds Force Commander Soleimani flew to Moscow to enlist Russian support for a counter-offensive to salvage the Syrian regime, these flights to Syria actually increased. And so last year your colleague at Treasury testified that regardless of the deal, a foreign bank that conducts or facilitates a significant financial transaction with Iran's Mahan Air will risk losing its access to U.S. financial systems.

So, instead of more action to ground these planes as part of a prisoner deal, the White House agreed to lift an Interpol Red Notice against Mahan's chief executive and a senior manager whom the U.S. Treasury said was responsible for the airline's sanctions evasions operations. So if we are serious, we could take immediate action against those financial institutions that transact on this Iranian airline's behalf in Asia and Europe and the Gulf, we should slap heavy fines on European and Asian ground service companies working with the airlines. Are we going to do that?

Mr. SMITH. Sir, we have been very engaged around the world on the question of Mahan Air. We have reminded our allies, our partners and other third countries of the secondary sanctions that remain with respect to Mahan Air.

We have continued to designate those entities that try to support Mahan Air around the world. We did some designations several months ago. We continue to look at those targets.

And we continue to engage with governments around the world on the need to stop working with Mahan Air. And we are going after the finances where we can. Yes, indeed.

Chairman ROYCE. Yes, but I have just got to point out, so unless those heavy fines—I mean it is one thing to jawbone and to say this—but in the meantime they are expanding their operations. And in the meantime they are flying into Syria on a regular basis. And you see what is happening in Aleppo in terms of the encirclement of Aleppo. As that support comes in it has very dire consequences in Syria.

And what I don't see is the push-back.

Let me give you another example. So what is the specific national security interest that justifies this claimed waiver? We know what happened. We passed legislation here that said you don't get an automatic visa waiver. You have got to go through the regular process so that we can check if you go to Syria or you go to Iran or you go to Sudan, because those are state sponsors of terrorism. By what logic does the administration then do a carve-out? What is this national security interest that justifies this waiver?

Does the U.S. have a national security interest in supporting so-called legitimate business in Iran? This is the argument the administration makes. Legitimate business in Iran, the reality is, as your

Treasury Department says, the Revolutionary Guard Corps is the most powerful economic actor. How does this justify going around the law that the President signed simply because the Iranian's protested this?

Mr. SMITH. Sir, I can say that with respect to the Iranian Revolutionary Guard Corps, secondary sanctions continue to attach. We continue to enforce those.

With respect to the Visa Waiver Program, I would have to defer to my colleagues at the State Department.

Chairman ROYCE. Well, let me expand, explain, Ambassador and Mr. Smith. What the administration should have told Iran is stop supporting terrorism and this won't be a problem. Because the way we wrote it is "state sponsors of terrorism." But the problem we are having is that Iran has not changed its course. Iran is still supporting Hezbollah to the hilt, still saying they are going to transfer 100,000, 100,000 GPS guidance systems to help missiles and rockets held by Hezbollah—provided by Iran, by the way—to better target cities inside Israel.

But instead of doing that, instead of taking that stance, you created an exception, the administration created an exception. And, again, the President signed the law. It sounds harsh, but it sure looks as if the Supreme Leader effectively vetoed the bill that had been passed and signed.

Ambassador MULL. Mr. Chairman, the administration supported the law, that legislation as it came through the Congress, to amend requirements for the Visa Waiver Program as a means of tightening the security of our borders, which is something very important to the administration.

That law, the Congress included in that law a waiver provision to allow waivers for those cases that affected the national security of the United States. As a government, in implementing that law we have to develop what the criteria are for exercising what those waivers will be.

And I can tell you that none of the criteria that we considered was how to promote greater business engagement with Iran. It was really aimed at making sure that those people who carry out important missions to our national security in Iran, whether it is the IAEA inspectors who need to get into Iran to verify that Iran is keeping its commitments, or to allow journalists to go in and report——

Chairman ROYCE. That, that was not our objection. Our objection is that the administration turned the concept of a case by case waiver on its head. Under the law, the proper question is, why is it in the national security interests of the United States that this particular person be allowed to enter the United States without a visa?

But you have boiled that down to, is this person involved in so-called legitimate business in Iran, at a time when the IRGC controls all the major businesses in Iran? A broad category that was expressly discussed and then rejected during the legislative process.

We had this debate. We had this debate with the administration. We reached our consensus. This bill was signed into law and then the Iranians objected. They objected because they wanted more business with the IRGC and with these other entities controlled by the mullahs and controlled by the Iranian Revolutionary Guard Corps.

I should go to Mr. Engel. My time has expired. But thank you very much, Ambassador and Mr. Smith.

Mr. ENGEL. Thank you, Mr. Chairman.

I think what you are hearing is the frustration that while we seem to be in many instances talking tough about Iran, in reality we are, our actions are far away from our rhetoric. And that is a worrisome thing. We want to make sure that Iran's feet are held to the fire. And we don't want loopholes to allow Iran to wiggle out of the thing, wiggle out of their obligations.

Let me ask, Ambassador Mull, the administration said that on Implementation Day Iran would receive around $50 billion. And the government spokesman in Iran claimed $100 billion was released. Do we know exactly how much was released and where the money is going?

Ambassador MULL. Our estimate really throughout this process has been that Iran had slightly upwards of $100 billion in frozen assets in international financial institutions around the world. Of that amount, a significant portion of it, our understanding is more than $50 billion, is already tied up and committed to other debts, to trade deals that had stalled because of those frozen assets. And that, in fact, those assets really available of that slightly upwards of $100 billion, about $50 billion would be available. That has remained our assessment throughout.

Mr. ENGEL. Thank you.

Mr. Smith, President Rouhani recently toured Europe. And in doing so, he is seeking to deepen economic ties, particularly it seems to me between Iran and Italy and Iran and France. He announced tens of billions of dollars in new economic ventures.

Are we expecting that Europe will hold a hard line on the deal should Iran cheat, or I should say when Iran cheats? Do we expect Europe to enforce snap back sanctions if Iran cheats, when now it is becoming economically beneficial to have some of the European countries having these deals with Iran? How much can we count on them if and when Iran cheats—and I suspect that they will— that Europe will forego some of its ventures and slap economic sanctions on Iran?

Mr. SMITH. Sir, I fully expect that Europe is going to continue to remain a committed partner with us and our sanctions programs. We have to remember that Europe had many of these trade deals before 2010, before 2012, and yet Europe has gone along with us. They have already sacrificed many of those deals the first time around and cut those deals off in compliance with the coordination that we have done and the secondary sanctions that we have implemented in cooperation with this Congress.

So I fully expect that Europe will continue to comply with the deal that we have struck.

Mr. ENGEL. But the lifting of the arms embargo and the lifting of the sanction against—sanctions against Iran's ballistic missile program obviously could further destabilize the region. When the arms embargo expires, Iran will legally be able to ship weapons to Assad, to Hamas, to Hezbollah, and international interdiction efforts will suffer greatly. And after 8 years, countries will be able to sell Iran components for its ballistic missile program.

It's galling, because during the entire negotiations we were told that the only thing that was being negotiated was not ballistic missile programs, just the nuclear question. And then suddenly we find this, this clause stuck in which allows and frees Iran from being banned from purchasing ballistic missiles in 8 years, and others in 5 years.

So how will U.S. sanctions work to address this issue after 5 years and after 8 years?

Mr. SMITH. I think part of the reason that you saw the difference in what the U.N. would allow after years was the way that we had all conceived of our sanctions. I think the U.N. had looked at those sanctions, and those sanctions were imposed at the U.N. and we got the U.N. consensus because those were viewed as nuclear-related sanctions. So they were viewed at the U.N. level as part of the nuclear-related file.

But I will tell you that the U.S. sanctions, our secondary sanctions, continue with respect to the ballistic missile program. We have all of the major Iranian components related to the ballistic missile program on our SDN List. Secondary sanctions remain on those individuals and entities. Which means that any European or third country or other actor that deals with Iran and deals with those entities with respect to the ballistic missile program, even after 8 years, will still have to contend with our secondary sanctions.

Mr. ENGEL. Let me, let me ask you my final question. What has the response been from our allies in the Middle East since Implementation Day? That would include Israel and the Sunni Arab countries. What is the administration doing to reach out to Israel and our Gulf allies, those who are obviously more closely affected by the Iran deal, to raise their comfort level?

Ambassador MULL. Thank you, Ranking Member Engel. In my current capacity, since taking on this responsibility in September I have met several times with senior Israeli officials to hear their concerns. Secretary Kerry also maintains a regular dialog, not only with the Israeli leadership but also with our Gulf allies, on a regular basis to address their concerns.

It is no secret that Israel was opposed to this deal. My impression since the deal came into force is that they want to work with us to make sure that it is implemented fully. That is a partnership and a relationship that I welcome.

I intend to go to Israel in the next few weeks to continue that dialog. Secretary Kerry most recently was in Riyadh to meet with his counterparts from the GCC states to hear their concerns. They have been supportive of the deal as well, but they also want us to remain focused on Iran's destabilizing activity in the region. And, of course, we will be.

Mr. ENGEL. Thank you, gentlemen.

Thank you, Madam Chair.

Ms. ROS-LEHTINEN [presiding]. Thank you, Ranking Member Engel.

In the 1990s previous CIA directors confirmed in Congressional testimony that North Korea was selling missiles and technology to

Iran. In 2013 former State Department Official David Asher testified before our committee that a cooperation agreement signed in 2002 between North Korea and Iran was the ''keystone''—his phrase—for the North Korea designated nuclear reactor built by Iran proxy Syria, which was destroyed in 2007.

And throughout the years there have been a litany of reports confirming Iran/North Korea collaboration on nuclear and ballistic missile technology, as well as the presence of Iranian and North Korean scientists and technicians at the test of these weapons in their respective countries. The United States has repeatedly sanctioned North Korean and Iranian entities for their collaboration on these issues.

Reports now indicate that Iranian scientists were again present for North Korea's nuclear test in January. So I have several questions related to that.

Ambassador Mull, what U.S. entities are tasked with monitoring Iranian/North Korean collaboration on nuclear and ballistic missile issues?

And if Iran acquires nuclear technical knowledge from North Korea, and just the expertise, the know-how, the results of the nuclear test, not actual nuclear-related materials, would Iran be in violation of the JCPOA or any other sanctions against itself or North Korea?

And, also, can you confirm if Iranian officials, scientists, or technicians were present in North Korea for its latest nuclear detonation on January 6th?

And moving to another topic under the JCPOA's Annex 3, the civil nuclear cooperation, the U.S. and other P5+1 members are obligated to cooperate in helping Iran develop its civil nuclear program. Has the U.S. or any other P5+1 country begun any transfers to Iran as part of this annex? And what has been transferred? How do we reconcile some of these transfers with prohibitions under existing U.S. law?

And, lastly, the U.S. no longer seems to care as much about Iran's human rights atrocities and its support for terrorism worldwide because the administration seems solely fixed on giving Iran a good report card on complying with the nuclear deal. If you could comment on that as well?

Thank you, gentlemen.

Ambassador MULL. Congresswoman, thank you very much for those very topical questions which I will be happy to address.

You are right that through the years there have been connections with Iran with many other parties—North Korea but others as well—in developing the nuclear program that we find, have found to be such a great threat against our interests, interests of Israel and our other friends in the region.

So that is the reason that we took on this deal, to limit the capacity for that program to pose a threat.

Ms. ROS-LEHTINEN. So which are the entities that are tasked with monitoring this? Which are they?

Ambassador MULL. Yes. So I can assure you, there are few issues that get as much attention in the U.S. intelligence community, our diplomatic attention, our military attention than the nuclear threats from Iran, North Korea and elsewhere. We will remain very much engaged, in fact, I would say even more engaged now that we have very specific criteria by which to judge Iran's compliance with this agreement.

Ms. ROS-LEHTINEN. But can you confirm whether Iranian officials were present in North Korea?

Ambassador MULL. I cannot.

Ms. ROS-LEHTINEN. Okay.

Ambassador MULL. I will be happy to look into that.

Ms. ROS-LEHTINEN. And if, if they acquire—if Iran gets from North Korea not the actual materials but a lot of the expertise, would that be a violation under JCPOA?

Ambassador MULL. The JCPOA spells out very specific measurable commitments that Iran must meet: The number of centrifuges, the number of enriched material that it has, the extent of its reactor program.

Ms. ROS-LEHTINEN. But if, if Iran gets know-how, advice, et cetera, results from tests but not material itself, is that a violation?

Ambassador MULL. North Korea is not specifically mentioned in the agreement. However, in the agreement Iran committed to refraining from all research aimed at developing a nuclear weapon. If we had reason to believe they were not complying with that, we have all the full range of our previous——

Ms. ROS-LEHTINEN. And then just quickly, have we begun any transfers to Iran on this, the Annex, the 3rd Annex, the civil nuclear cooperation?

Ambassador MULL. That annex does not require civil nuclear cooperation. It allows, as appropriate. The United States has not provided any material. However, we will be co-chairing a working group of the P5+1 that will review Iran's development of a new Arak reactor to make sure that it does not——

Ms. ROS-LEHTINEN. Mr. Smith, just one note. You are not overlooking the human rights record, you're not overlooking their support for terrorism throughout the region, throughout the world?

Mr. SMITH. No, ma'am. We continue to be very engaged in Iran's human rights abuses and its support for terrorism. We have already designated many of the principal actors in Iran, many of the principal entities that have engaged in human rights abuses. And we continue to follow the evidence.

Ms. ROS-LEHTINEN. Thank you, sir.

Mr. Deutch of Florida.

Mr. DEUTCH. Thank you very much, Madam Chairman.

I want to touch on three, three different things. Thanks for being here. I want to talk about the $100 billion in frozen assets that are now available to Iran.

I want to talk about the secondary sanctions, U.S. secondary sanctions on ballistic missiles, and sanctions under the deal.

And, third, I want to talk about non-nuclear sanctions and in the 300 individuals and entities that were de-listed on Implementation Day.

So, first, on the issue of the funds, Ambassador Mull, you explained that the $100 billion, that $50 billion is tied up elsewhere and then $50 billion is available. Whatever the ultimate numbers are, what are we doing to actually track that money as it is released, since any of that money that flows into the hands of those who are supporting terrorists would then trigger terrorist sanctions or human rights sanctions?

Ambassador MULL. In this setting I can tell you that we monitor it very closely, without going into too many details, where those assets go as they are released. As General Clapper testified earlier, a few days ago, so far it seems that most of those funds are going into infrastructure, domestic infrastructure projects to the extent that they are able to monitor that.

But we have not seen a substantial change in levels of support for terrorist actively. However, we remain very closely focused on that. And through the sanctions that we have remaining, a very strong toolkit of sanctions, we remain ready to take appropriate, exact appropriate penalties when required.

Mr. DEUTCH. Good. I hope that—I appreciate that response and I hope that we have an opportunity to continue to engage in this discussion in this setting and in a classified setting.

Secondly, on the issue of ballistic missiles, Mr. Smith, you talk about U.S. secondary sanctions applying even after 8 years. I am less concerned now about what happens after 8 years than I am about what is happening right now. And right now Iran has violated U.N. Security Council resolutions by testing those ballistic missiles.

We have imposed sanctions. And I commend the administration for doing so. But the JCPOA, the international component of the JCPOA is founded upon a Security Council resolution. What, if anything, can we expect the Security Council to do in response to the clear violations of existing Security Council resolutions and the JCPOA that Iran has engaged in by testing these missiles?

Mr. SMITH. So what I can tell you is that we still have most of the major economic actors in Iran that have engaged in ballistic missile testing and any of the work on that, we still have them on our secondary sanctions list.

Mr. DEUTCH. No, I understand. The Security Council.

Mr. SMITH. In terms of the Security Council activity, I would probably defer to my State colleague.

Ambassador MULL. And that is, will the Security Council remain focused on——

Mr. DEUTCH. We took these tests to the Security Council, as I understand it. The Security Council looked at it. Then it goes to the Sanctions Committee.

Where does it stand now? How likely is it that we are actually going to see sanctions on what is a clear violation of the U.N. Security Council resolution? And, if they don't sanction when there is a clear violation, what confidence can we have in their ability to carry out the terms of the JCPOA?

Ambassador MULL. Well, the Security Council, of course, has a feature that was written into the founding treaty of the Security Council where permanent members of the Security Council have a veto. So, and we had raised in days after this test our strong belief, Ambassador Power condemned this launch as a violation of U.N. Security Council 1929, which we believe. The Sanctions Committee agreed with that assessment.

Mr. DEUTCH. Okay.

Ambassador MULL. The Security Council has not yet won the full agreement of all five permanent members to take appropriate actions. But I will tell you, Congressman, we don't counter the Iranian missile program just by relying on the Security Council. We have a broad range of tools that we can use for this.

Mr. DEUTCH. Ambassador, no, no, I understand that. And I appreciate that. But it gets back to my main point here which is under the terms of the JCPOA there is—we wrapped all of these Security Council resolutions into a new Security Council resolution that specifically includes the ballistic missile section, which has now been violated. And, ultimately, we have been told throughout, including this morning, that our allies remain committed. Which this, I guess the question is, is that just simply our closest allies? Is it no longer the P5+1? That is a concern.

But I only have a little time left. And I would just like to turn to my last issue which is, the companies that, the 300 individuals and entities that were de-listed on Implementation Day, we have been told repeatedly that that list is being scrubbed, and that if any one of those individuals or entities should be sanctioned for violating either the terrorism—either because they export terrorism or because they violate human rights, that they would be sanctioned.

Where are we on the review? Have you identified any who should be? And when will those sanctions be applied?

Ambassador MULL. Congressman, we, actually even before we reached Implementation Day, although we have agreed to remove 400 entities from the so-called SDN List because of their being put there for nuclear reasons, on Implementation Day while removing them for the nuclear reasons, we added 200 of those back onto our SDN List because of terrorism and other, other concerns.

I can ask Mr. Smith to get into the details.

Mr. SMITH. So what I can say is that when we took the 400 off, before we did that we did the comprehensive review of all of them to make sure that we were comfortable with removing them. But if we saw any support for terrorism, human rights abuses, ballistic missiles, we kept those entities on.

Since that time we have continued to follow the evidence. If there is evidence of any kind of activity that would violate our sanctions that fall within the sanctions that remain, we will act against those actively.

Mr. DEUTCH. I understand. But if I can just clarify. So are you say—because this is, I didn't know this. You are saying that of the 400 individuals and entities who were listed in the agreement, 200 of them are still being sanctioned for terrorism and human rights violations?

Mr. SMITH. No. I should clarify this. As we removed 400 from the list because they were not related to terrorism, human rights abuses, ballistic missiles or others, 200 of those were marked by the Treasury Department before as Government of Iran or Iranian financial institution. We still in the United States, our U.S. persons are still obligated to block and do no transactions with anyone that is identified as the Government of Iran or the Iranian financial institution.

So those 200 that we put on a separate list, just a list for U.S. persons to say these are Government of Iran or Iranian financial institutions, no terrorism, no human rights abuse.

Mr. DEUTCH. Which I understand. I just want to know have you—where are you in scrubbing the list of other names? And when will you make a determination whether any of those other individuals or entities should be subject to sanctions for terrorism or human rights violations?

Mr. SMITH. So the plan that we continue to have is that we review all of the intel and all of the evidence that comes in. We don't look at every name that is on our—we have 5,000 names on our SDN List—we don't look at every name. We look at all of the intel that comes in to see, does that affect any name on our SDN List? Should we add a name for our SDN List?

So we work with our IC partners and the rest of the U.S. Government to make sure we collect all the information, and if it is sanctionable conduct, whether or not you were removed from our list or you were never on our list, that is when we take action.

Mr. DEUTCH. Has any action been taken?

Mr. SMITH. We have taken action. We took action the day after Implementation Day against a number of ballistic missile supporters. We continue to work. We designated an al-Qaeda-related entity yesterday.

We are continuing to work across the range of our sanctions programs.

Mr. SMITH OF NEW JERSEY [presiding]. The time of the gentleman has expired. The chair recognizes himself.

My understanding is on the ballistic missile deal, they are relatively low-level people. Let me ask you with regard to the—and a simple yes or no would be very helpful—the Iran Sanctions Act expires, as you know, on December 31st of this year. Will the administration support legislation simply extending the Iran Sanctions Act so that nuclear-related sanctions it provides can be snapped back if Iran cheats?

I know there has been some talk already that talk of that is premature. I absolutely disagree. We need to set this as just a straight reauthorization for it.

Secondly, in terms of enriched uranium, exactly what can—and, Ambassador Mull, this will be to you, of course—what can 5,060 centrifuge machines actually produce? Does it constitute any threat whatsoever? And if they build more machines, how can we be sure that that has or has not happened?

You have testified that Iran shipped almost all of its estimated uranium stockpile out of the country, leaving behind no more than 300 kilograms over 15 years in Iran. Could you tell us exactly where Iran's enriched uranium has been shipped? Who watches it? Who guards it? And is there any potential or any concern that it could be clandestinely returned to Iran?

And, of course, I have raised this with Secretary Kerry in the past, are there concerns that North Korea could be providing such materials to Iran in a clandestine way?

And, finally, on the human rights issue, and I am going to be chairing in my subcommittee another hearing on human rights issues in Iran, they are despicable. It is one of the worst violators of human rights in the entire world. The use of torture, the use of executions, there are very few parallels. North Korea comes to mind, and a few other countries. How many individuals have been designated? Has the top Justice in Iran been designated?

And we yield for your answers.

Mr. SMITH. I will start with the last question on human rights abuses. We have continued to designate under human rights authority. But we designated all of the top actors in Iran almost from the beginning. And so if you go down the list on human rights, we have got the IRGC, we have got the Iranian Ministry of Intelligence and Security. We have got all of the major, the law enforcement forces, the Iranian Cyber Police, the Center to Investigate Organized Crime. All of the major actors in Iran that would have any involvement with human rights abuses, we have designated.

The numbers are about 37 individuals and entities that have been designated because we went after all of the big, big actors.

Mr. SMITH OF NEW JERSEY. How many in the past year?

Mr. SMITH. None in the past year because we had already——

Mr. SMITH OF NEW JERSEY. I see.

Mr. SMITH [continuing]. We had already done the major actors before that time.

Mr. SMITH OF NEW JERSEY. And what is the consequence of such a designation in your terms?

Mr. SMITH. The assets are frozen in the United States. U.S. persons are prevented from dealing with them.

But it also carries the secondary sanctions, so we can tell third country entities, you deal with these individuals or entities you——

Mr. SMITH OF NEW JERSEY. And the response of those third country entities?

Mr. SMITH. If Europe tries to deal with any of those that are designated human rights abusers, I mean I would say that Europe has many of those actors still remaining on its sanctions list, so we haven't see that conduct. But we would go to anyone and say, you will be cut off from the United States if you continue to deal with those actors.

Mr. SMITH OF NEW JERSEY. And you are ready to do that. Have you done that yet?

Mr. SMITH. We haven't seen that activity. Those organizations and individuals are not the ones that anyone is trying to deal with at this time.

Mr. SMITH OF NEW JERSEY. Ambassador Mull.

Ambassador MULL. Sir, on your nuclear-related questions, the 5,060 centrifuges, IR–1 centrifuges that are permitted to operate, the operational part of the agreement isn't on what they produce, it is that Iran may not have more than 300 kilograms at any time in the next 15 years of no more than 3.67 percent relatively low enriched uranium. If Iran exceeds that amount, it will face a response from the Joint Commission which could feature being declared in violation of the agreement, and then appropriate snapback sanctions that could take—that would be one of the consequences.

Secondly, if Iran builds or employs more than 5,060 centrifuges, they will also be subject to being declared in violation of the agreement. These enrichment facilities are under 24/7 monitoring by the

IAEA, with cameras, with regular visits. And we have a good handle on whether or not they will be keeping those commitments.

In terms of other covert support, because there is full-time IAEA monitoring of the entire fuel cycle within Iran, it is impossible to introduce elements into that system without being detected by the system, by the IAEA. That applies to whether North Korea supplies material or anyone.

The material that Iran shipped out, that 25,000 pounds of nuclear, enriched nuclear material, Russia took that under its control. We obviously have many differences over many years with Russia, but one of the features of our relationship is pretty close cooperation on protection of nuclear material. We do not have concerns that that material——

Mr. SMITH OF NEW JERSEY. Do we have any on site accountability? Can we go and verify ourselves or?

Ambassador MULL. We cannot.

Mr. SMITH OF NEW JERSEY. We cannot. Who does?

Ambassador MULL. Well, we—I mean Russia has tons of nuclear material and has for many years. Russia is responsible for maintaining access and controls.

Mr. SMITH OF NEW JERSEY. What town is it actually being— where is the repository for it?

Ambassador MULL. I'm sorry?

Mr. SMITH OF NEW JERSEY. Where has it been put?

Ambassador MULL. It has not been fully, according to our information it has not yet been decided where exactly Russia will put this.

Mr. SMITH OF NEW JERSEY. Because if it has been shipped out it has gone somewhere. It's not——

Ambassador MULL. It is still in the process of being delivered in its entirety.

Mr. SMITH OF NEW JERSEY. So it is not all shipped out yet?

Ambassador MULL. It is all shipped out. It all left Iran on a ship.

Mr. SMITH OF NEW JERSEY. But where did it go? I mean it has to be somewhere.

Ambassador MULL. It is on a Russian ship, in Russian custody, under Russian control.

Mr. SMITH OF NEW JERSEY. Actually on the ship right now?

Ambassador MULL. I believe, if it has not arrived yet, it will very soon. And it will be kept within control of Russian facilities.

Mr. SMITH OF NEW JERSEY. But again, we are then trusting the Russians to say that they have it under their purview, that they are watching it? I mean they are so close to Iran, they have doubledealed us and especially the Middle East, the Syrians, I don't know why we would trust them. Could you tell us where it is going? I mean that is important. And then I will——

Ambassador MULL. That is a Russian Government responsibility to decide where it goes. We do not have concerns about Russian custody of this material. What is important in this deal is will it go back to Iran? And I can guarantee there are sufficient controls in place that if one piece of dust of that material goes back into Iran we are going to be aware of it.

Mr. SMITH OF NEW JERSEY. But again, can the IAEA go to that ship and verify that it is there and follow it as it goes to its final resting place?

Ambassador MULL. IAEA has different monitoring arrangements with each, each country in the world.

Mr. SMITH OF NEW JERSEY. I would not have confidence that— I mean it is not even in a place, it is not in any city that you say. It is not in any, it is not somewhere in Russia that we could say there it is. We don't even know where it is.

Ambassador MULL. The IAEA verified the loading of all of this material onto the——

Mr. SMITH OF NEW JERSEY. But loading and where does it end up is very important.

Ambassador MULL. That is the Russian Government's responsibility to decide where it goes.

Mr. SMITH OF NEW JERSEY. That is a flaw, in my opinion.

And the yes or no on the Iran Sanctions Act?

Ambassador MULL. On the Iran Sanctions Act we are, you know, we remain ready to work with the committee to decide on when and if it should be properly reauthorized.

Mr. SMITH OF NEW JERSEY. I think it is our opinion, many of us, not everyone, is that if you want snap-back sanctions and you want to continue the accountability regimen you have got to have the Iran Sanctions Act. I don't know why it is not a simple yes. I think we are talking about straight reauthorization.

Brad Sherman.

Mr. SHERMAN. The entire country has been captivated by ISIS. The beheadings on YouTube provoked us all. But the Shiite extremist alliance based in Tehran is more dangerous and more evil. They have killed far more Americans, hundreds in the 1980s in Lebanon, hundreds in Iraq and hundreds in Afghanistan, from Iranian-provided IEDs.

This alliance of Iran, Assad, Hezbollah and the Houthi is racking up victories in the Middle East now. They are not just more evil because they kill more—they killed more Americans. They are responsible for the deaths of 200,000 Syrian civilians. The difference here is that Assad, supported by Iran, and by the money that Iran now has available, when ISIS kills 50 people they put it on YouTube, when Assad kills 100, kills thousands he has the good taste to deny it.

Now, this nuclear deal was not supposed to be a ''get out of jail free card'' for everything that Iran does. We have our Section 301 and Section 302 of the Iran Threat Reduction Act that I worked with our former and present chairman on. You have only designated 70 entities under 301. But just as important, under 302 you have not sanctioned a single business that I can identify, for doing business with the Iran Revolutionary Guard Corps, an entity that puts new blood on its hands every day in Syria.

Mr. Smith, what is the most prominent or well-known company that has been sanctioned for doing business under Section 302, for doing business with the Iran Revolutionary Guard Corps.

Mr. SMITH. Sir, I am sorry, I would have to get you that information.

Mr. SHERMAN. I got the information: Zero point zero.

Mr. SMITH. We have done a significant amount of IRGC designations. IRGC is the——

Mr. SHERMAN. Designations are nice. What about sanctions?

Mr. SMITH. Designations are sanctions, sir. Designations under this accord——

Mr. SHERMAN. I am talking about secondary sanctions.

Mr. SMITH. So when we designate an IRGC, you have the IRGC label on our Web site then if we designate that you have that——

Mr. SHERMAN. Okay, look, the IRGC isn't trying to do business in the United States. The IRGC is getting its supplies from companies in Europe. Which European companies have you sanctioned for doing business with the Iran Revolutionary Guard Corps.

Mr. SMITH. When we designate an IRGC and we put an IRGC tag, that carries secondary sanctions.

Mr. SHERMAN. Have you imposed these secondary sanctions, Mr. Smith, or can you just—the filibustering is supposed to go over on the Senate side.

Mr. SMITH. The answer is if they carry secondary sanctions——

Mr. SHERMAN. Have you designated, have you imposed a secondary sanction on any business in Europe?

Mr. SMITH. We do not have to because the European actors have moved away from that business.

Mr. SHERMAN. And none of them are doing business with the IRGC?

Mr. SMITH. I have not seen evidence of European actors continuing to deal with the IRGC.

Mr. SHERMAN. Okay. What about South Asian and East Asian actors?

Mr. SMITH. I haven't seen——

Mr. SHERMAN. Nobody is doing it? Okay, because the Treasury Department has announced that the IRGC is this huge economic monolith. You have only designated 70; there are lot more fronts for you to designate. But you say it is this huge economic, and yet you can't find a single East Asian, South Asian or European company that is doing business with them.

Let me move on to Air Mahan, another designated entity, the airline of choice for the Iran Revolutionary Guard Corps and for thugs going to Syria to kill people. They are flying Airbus aircraft into friendly countries in the Middle East and Europe. That, those Airbus aircraft have U.S. technology on it. What have we done to prevent those aircraft from being received in those friendly cities?

Mr. SMITH. A number of agencies of the U.S. Government, including Treasury, Commerce, State, and others, have been actively engaged to try to prevent Mahan Air from being able to fly.

Mr. SHERMAN. Have we stopped anything or are we just sending letters?

Mr. SMITH. We have stopped.

Mr. SHERMAN. Where have we stopped Mahan?

Mr. SMITH. I don't think I can say in this setting. But I——

Mr. SHERMAN. Can you get that to me confidentially?

Mr. SMITH. Yes.

Mr. SHERMAN. We haven't—let's face it, they are flying into an awful lot of European and Asian and Middle East friendly cities.

Why haven't we nailed a single bank for doing business with Mahan? No secondary sanctions on any bank?

Mr. SMITH. We continue to try. We continue to do what we can to follow the——

Mr. SHERMAN. But we can't find a single bank that is doing business with Mahan?

Mr. SMITH. If we find the evidence, then we will go after them.

Mr. SHERMAN. Okay. But you have found zero evidence of any—I mean we are relying on the Executive Branch to enforce this deal because you are able to monitor what Iran does. And here is an example where you can't—you have got a major airline doing business in dozens of cities, and you can't find them doing business with a single bank.

Ms. ROS-LEHTINEN [presiding]. Thank you, Mr. Sherman. Thank you. Mr. Rohrabacher.

Mr. ROHRABACHER. Thank you very much.

First of all, I would like to associate myself with the concerns about human rights that Congressman Smith outlined. And I, I would like to say that there are ways of approaching the human rights issue that will have an impact for today. There are other ways, other ways of approaching it that will have a major impact for the future as well.

Let me just say that we have with us today folks in their yellow jackets who remind us. They are here as testimony to the fact that we have a brutal human rights abusing regime in Tehran. They are here to remind us that they have families and there are still people, whether it is in Camp Liberty or whether it is in Iran itself, who are being held and being tortured and being repressed by this Mullah government that has the destiny—they have the, how do they say, the blessings of God for these horrible crimes that they are committing against their own people, and have been doing so for decades now.

If we are to have a nuclear-free Iran, and what we are really trying to do is trying to stop this—we recognize now the Shiite/Sunni split, and the last thing we want to see is a nuclear exchange between Sunni Muslims and Shiite Muslims. This is really almost a human—not just for our own national security—it is almost a humanitarian effort on our part to try to prevent that weapons system become part of that historic fight between these two factions of Islam.

But let me just note that just the sanctions for human rights abuses is not enough. And I don't believe that we are doing it with the gusto or with the determination that we need to, although you know more about that than I do, what the potential use of this is. But that is one part of the human rights approach.

The other approach is that we need to be supporting those people, we are not just punishing those people who are oppressing the population, but supporting those people in the population who want to bring about a more democratic Iran and want to, basically, sever the Mullahs from their iron grip that they have on Iranian society.

Have we done anything, based on the fact that now we have had this rapprochement on the nuclear issue with the Iranian agreement, have we in any way stepped up support, direct support for any group within Iran that is trying to make a more democratic country?

Ambassador MULL. Congressman, thanks for the question. I am afraid I will have to take that back for you. In my responsibilities day to day, my job is focused exclusively on making sure Iran meets all of its commitments, that it doesn't get to have a nuclear weapons capability.

We remain gravely concerned about the human situation, human rights situation in Iran. I think there is probably not another country in the world who speaks up more often about our concern and takes action through the international community, through international organizations, as well as through our own laws and authorities.

Mr. ROHRABACHER. I am sorry, you folks wouldn't understand, wouldn't know if we had operations going on this part of the human rights issue, I mean challenging those people who are challenging human rights and versus helping those people, like the MEK and others, who are trying to overthrow this Mullah dictatorship and which would create a better situation for achieving all of our goals if we had a more democratic government there.

Let me just say that that is, if we do not do that, if we do not help those people who are struggling to build a more democratic Iran, we are just postponing the time when Iran and the Mullahs will have a nuclear weapon. Because our treaty that we are talking about, how many years is it before it no longer applies? Is it a 15-year event?

So instead of postponing, we don't need to postpone that time. We have already postponed it long enough. We need to eliminate that eventuality by making sure that we are supporting the democratic elements, like the MEK and others, and the Baluchs and the Azaris and others, and the Kurds in Iran, who want to live a more free society.

So thank you very much, Madam Chairman.

Ms. ROS-LEHTINEN. Thank you very much, Mr. Rohrabacher.

Mr. Connolly of Virginia.

Mr. CONNOLLY. Thank you, Madam Chairman.

You know it is really, this is a fascinating hearing because it is supposed to be on the implementation of the Iran nuclear deal. And some of the most strident and loud critics of entering into that deal at all are now focused on airlines and Revolutionary Guard business activities and sanctions and closing up banks and rather than the actual elements of the nuclear agreement, which they were the first to say would never work. They would cheat. The metrics weren't good enough. This was enabling nuclear development by Iran.

So, Ambassador Mull, I am going to ask some questions about the nuclear agreement and its compliance. So any evidence of Iran cheating so far?

Ambassador MULL. So far, no. I can tell you, Congressman, that in the 6 months or so I have been working on this in the run-up to Implementation Day, whenever we detected that there might be a potential for moving away from the commitments we have engaged with our Iranian counterparts and they have addressed those concerns every single time.

Mr. CONNOLLY. Every single time. Okay.

Ambassador MULL. Yes.

Mr. CONNOLLY. We are going to have to run through this real quickly because I want to try to understand.

Let me see. One of the requirements of the agreement was to modify the Arak heavy water research reactor so that it could no longer produce weapons grade plutonium; is that correct?

Ambassador MULL. Yes, that is correct.

Mr. CONNOLLY. And did they do that?

Ambassador MULL. Yes.

Mr. CONNOLLY. What did they do to do that?

Ambassador MULL. They removed the core of the reactor and filled it with concrete so it could not operate.

Mr. CONNOLLY. Is that reversible?

Ambassador MULL. Not very easily, no.

Mr. CONNOLLY. Is it observable?

Ambassador MULL. Yes, it was observed.

Mr. CONNOLLY. So they complied?

Ambassador MULL. Yes.

Mr. CONNOLLY. Pretty big deal?

Ambassador MULL. Yes.

Mr. CONNOLLY. All right. They had 19,000 estimated centrifuges. And they were required under the agreement to get down to 6,104; is that correct?

Ambassador MULL. That is right, sir.

Mr. CONNOLLY. Did they do that?

Ambassador MULL. Yes, sir, they did.

Mr. CONNOLLY. They did?

Ambassador MULL. Yes.

Mr. CONNOLLY. And was that observable?

Ambassador MULL. It was. It was verified by the IAEA.

Mr. CONNOLLY. Oh, my Lord. All right.

They had full enrichment at Natanz and Fordow. What is the status there?

Ambassador MULL. Natanz, enrichment at Natanz is proceeding, as allowed by the agreement. All enrichment operations at Fordow have been observably ceased.

Mr. CONNOLLY. And what was the enrichment level before the agreement?

Ambassador MULL. The highest amount that they enriched to was 19.75 percent.

Mr. CONNOLLY. 19.75; and is that weapons grade?

Ambassador MULL. No.

Mr. CONNOLLY. And but they are required to get down to 3.67; is that correct?

Ambassador MULL. Yes, sir.

Mr. CONNOLLY. So from 19 to less than 4?

Ambassador MULL. Yes.

Mr. CONNOLLY. Did they do that?

Ambassador MULL. Yes, sir.

Mr. CONNOLLY. Was that observable?

Ambassador MULL. Yes, it was.

Mr. CONNOLLY. Can they quickly go back to 20 or 19?

Ambassador MULL. Only by breaking elements of the agreement. And they would have to do so in places that are under the full-time observation of the IAEA.

Mr. CONNOLLY. Now did I understand you to say that their stockpile of enriched uranium was in excess of 25,000 kilograms?

Ambassador MULL. 25,000 pounds.

Mr. CONNOLLY. 25,000 pounds. And the agreement says they can have no more than 300 kilograms; is that correct?

Ambassador MULL. Yes, sir.

Mr. CONNOLLY. From 25,000 pounds to 300 kilograms. Did they do that?

Ambassador MULL. Yes, sir.

Mr. CONNOLLY. You are kidding?

Ambassador MULL. No.

Mr. CONNOLLY. They complied again?

Ambassador MULL. Yes.

Mr. CONNOLLY. And was that observable?

Ambassador MULL. It was observed and documented by the IAEA.

Mr. CONNOLLY. Hmmm. Now, they also had to agree that centrifuge production in the uranium mines and mills would be subject to IAEA international inspection at any time; is that correct?

Ambassador MULL. Yes, sir.

Mr. CONNOLLY. Have they complied with that?

Ambassador MULL. Yes, sir.

Mr. CONNOLLY. Huh. So all those predictions of the end of the world, Armageddon, the fact is we are just enabling the nuclear development, it sounds to me, Ambassador Mull, that at least so far we are not dealing with a perfect state, we are not dealing with perfect behavior, there are lots of other things we object to vehemently, but with respect to this agreement so far they have, in fact, abided by it. Not cheated that we know of. We have a pretty vigorous inspection regime. We have metrics they have met. And it sounds to me like, despite predictions to the contrary notwithstanding, they are further away from a nuclear weapon today than they were before the agreement. Is that correct? Would that be a fair assessment from your point of view?

Ambassador MULL. That is undeniably true.

Mr. CONNOLLY. Well, my Lord. So we can, you know, we can decide we want to pillory the administration in one of the most important nuclear agreements, in my opinion, in our lifetime. I happen to draw the opposite conclusion of the Prime Minister of Israel. The existential threat to Israel would have been denying this agreement.

It is hard work to make an agreement. It is hard work to make it implemented. It is hard work to validate it. It is hard work to stick with it and oversee it. But so far it is working. And thank God it is.

Ms. ROS-LEHTINEN. And it is hard work to say that is enough, Mr. Connolly.

And now we turn to Mr. Wilson.

Mr. WILSON. Thank you, Madam Chair. And I really appreciate the extraordinary efforts of Chairman Ed Royce's leadership to expose the increasing threats to American families by the Iran deal.

Additionally, I am really grateful this is a bipartisan concern. We have heard it from Ranking Member Engel, Mr. Deutch, Congressman Sherman.

And Ambassador Smith, Mull and Mr. Smith, I believe your testimony today confirms American families are at greater risk than ever, that the terrorists are better financed than ever to achieve their goal of death to America and death to Israel. And in fact, Mr. Smith, you admitted that Iran is a state sponsor of terrorism. How could you not recognize that by releasing $100 billion to a state sponsor of terrorism that a significant amount of that money would be used to kill American families?

Mr. SMITH. Sir, I think we thought that a state sponsor of terrorism with a nuclear weapon was a far more dangerous threat to the international community, its neighbors, and to the United States. What I can say is that we put, through the efforts of our sanctions, Iran is in a $½-trillion hole. And what we released allows Iran to have about $50 billlon, much of which it needs to stabilize its currency and to have any foreign trade whatsoever.

Mr. WILSON. And American families are at risk. In fact, last month in Baghdad it was Iranian-backed terrorists that kidnaped four Americans. And so they are not stopping. And they may be kidnapping today.

I have still not forgotten 283 U.S. Marines killed in Beirut by the Iranian regime. We should not forget that. I had two sons serve in Iraq. Every day they are at risk of IEDs provided by Iran. Dismissing this is incredible and putting American people at risk.

And, Ambassador Mull, you indicate that Israel now supports the agreement. This is in direct contradiction to every bit of information that we have received from the Israelis themselves. And so yes or no, does Israel support this or not?

Ambassador MULL. Congressman, as I said in my testimony, the Chief of Staff of the Israel Armed Forces has publicly said that the threat to Israel of a nuclear Iran has declined as a result of this agreement. Does that mean that the entire Israeli Government is happy with it? No. It is obvious they have had serious concerns about it. But at the same time——

Mr. WILSON. Again, yes or no. But it is, hey, in a democracy you will have, thank God Israel is a democracy so you will have good people agree and disagree.

And back again to the development of intercontinental ballistic missiles, Ambassador. There was virtually no response as Iran continues to do that. There is only one purpose for the ICBMs, as indicated by Congressman Engel, Congressman Deutch, and that is to develop a capability of nuclear weapons to strike America. Is there any other reason for ICBMs?

Ambassador MULL. Well, that is one of the reasons that we undertook to rid Iran of the ability to attach nuclear payloads to those missiles. Missiles, ICBM missiles can be used without nuclear payloads; that is why they are still a threat to us and our allies and why we are working hard against them.

Mr. WILSON. But, hey, but hey, the real use of an ICBM is to use with a nuclear capability, not to make some type of conventional attack. The American people are truly at risk. And for this to simultaneously occur is extraordinary to me, and there not be repercussions. And so over and over again we see the American people at risk.

And then when you identify the IAEA inspections, is it not true there is not an American on the inspection team?

Ambassador MULL. There are a number of Americans who work in the IAEA.

Mr. WILSON. But not on this team itself?

Ambassador MULL. Americans do not travel to Iran; that is correct.

Mr. WILSON. No. And what you have really described, and the American people need to know this, no Americans, no Canadians. What you are really describing is self-verification by the Iranians of their own existence. And so I really am saddened by what I hear today. And to me it just confirms what Lieutenant General Michael Flynn, the former Director of the Defense Intelligence Agency said, ''That the Middle East policy is one of willful ignorance.'' And it is willful ignorance that I think is putting the American families at risk. And I hope you will change course.

There has been over and over again requests for what has been done to enforce sanctions, to reinstate sanctions. I am really grateful to be working on legislation with Congressman Joe Kennedy—it is bipartisan—about zero tolerance for violations.

I yield back my time.

Ms. ROS-LEHTINEN. Thank you, Mr. Wilson.

Mr. CICILLLINE.

Mr. CICILLLINE. Thank you, Madam Chair. Thanks for calling this event.

I thank Ranking Member Engel for at the beginning of this hearing reminding us that this agreement has been approved and now we have the responsibility to be certain that it is being implemented properly and we prevent Iran from becoming a nuclear power. And I think when you think about it, as you said, Ambassador Mull, what the consequences would have been in our efforts to push back on Iran in a number of ways in the region because of their aggression and ongoing activity, it would be a very different scenario if we were required to push back on an Iran with nuclear capability and make, I think make a difficult situation even more dangerous.

So I have three very specific questions. When the United States began negotiating with Iran, the breakout time was a few weeks to a few months, according to most experts. That plant I would say would have enough enriched uranium to build a nuclear weapon. How far is Iran from breakout now as a result of this implementation?

Ambassador MULL. Sir, over the course of the last 3 months Iran has moved from breakout time of about 2 months to at least 1 year.

Mr. CICILLLINE. Okay. The International Atomic Energy Agency is being asked to do some significant work in terms of compliance with this agreement. And I actually wrote to the President about this, urging that we be certain that we provide additional resources to the IAEA to do this work.

I know that the administration's proposal provides a modest increase. But I think the IAEA has already indicated that it is not sufficient. Could you speak to the importance of making certain that we, in a bipartisan way, allocate sufficient resources, recognizing we don't fund the entire operation but that we need to financially request of IAEA so they can do the work that we are asking them or requiring them to do?

Ambassador MULL. Yes, sir. I am in regular contact with the Director General of the IAEA, Yukiya Amano, to affirm that he has sufficient resources for his agency to do a very important job that is vital, vital to our national security interests. And that he has assured me that in terms of the—its responsibilities for the nuclear program it is fully funded and has everything it needs for the rest of this year.

Obviously, we will continue and we very much welcome the Congress' bipartisan support for making sure that the IAEA is fully funded.

Mr. CICILLLINE. Well, and I think the request they made for Fiscal Year 2017 is an increase of $10.6 million. So I don't think that is reflected in the administration request, but I think many of us are very concerned and want to be certain that they have the resources that they need.

And, finally, I know there has been a lot of discussion about the snap-back provisions and non-compliance by Iran, for obviously the behavior of this country and its leaders give us lots of reason to expect there will be some non-compliance. And what I am interested in knowing is what work the administration has done to deal with violations of this agreement?

While some people have argued if there is even the slightest unintentional violation, the deal is off, that would obviously result in the deal which will prevent Iran from being a nuclear power from being abandoned, which doesn't give us the result we want, to allow Iran to pursue its nuclear ambitions. So there has to have been some conversation on what is the administration's position about minor violations of the agreement. Have we developed a grade of what those kinds of things were? Have we communicated those to our European allies? I know there is some discussion of zero tolerance if there is anything, the deal is completely abandoned.

I would just like to know your thoughts on that, what the administration is considering and how we should think about sending a very clear message to the Iranians that any violation of this comes with a punishment and a consequence, even if it doesn't ultimately mean we reject the entire deal?

Ambassador MULL. Yes, sir. I can tell you that the JCPOA allows quite a broad range of potential responses to violations or contradictions to the agreement that range from a partial reimposition of sanctions to full imposition of not only bilateral sanctions, but those from the European Union and the U.N. Security Council.

I am not sure that it would be helpful for me to speculate here in terms of what each individual violation or contradiction to the agreement would provoke because we think that uncertainty of response is something that is a diplomatic asset to us as we go forward. But I can tell you that, generally speaking, the gold standard for us in deciding how to respond it the breakout time that we talked about a few moments ago, that if Iran's breakout time diminishes below a year, we would consider that to be a very serious violation and work with our allies to have the appropriate response.

Mr. CICILLLINE. And, of course, communicating to the Iranians that it is the position of the United States that any violation will be addressed and punished in an appropriate way.

Ambassador MULL. Yes, sir.

Mr. CICILLLINE. There is no, you know, death by a thousand small cuts.

Ambassador MULL. Yes. Yes, sir. And I can assure you we are in daily contact with IAEA on their evaluation of the situation in terms of Iran's compliance.

Ms. ROS-LEHTINEN. Thank you, Mr. Cicilline.

Mr. CICILLLINE. I yield back my time.

Ms. ROS-LEHTINEN. Mr. Duncan is recognized.

Mr. DUNCAN. Thank you, Madam Chair.

First off, let me say that I hope history is right and sides with Mr. Connolly's comments more than history did with Neville Chamberlain's comments. And we will see. I hope that Iran continues to comply. I hope that they don't have a nuclear weapon because the consequences are dire.

I want to talk about the Visa Waiver Program law that was passed as part of the Omnibus in 2015, December, as it relates to the JCPOA. And I specifically want to point to negotiations that went on from November 30th through the passage of the Omnibus.

These were negotiations between the White House, State Department, Homeland Security, and Members of the House and Senate. During—on November 30th, DHS asked for certain waivers for people to travel to Iran and Iraq in the post-March 2011 forward time frame. And the negotiations went on for quite some time. On November the 1st—excuse me, December the 1st, December the 1st, December the 2nd, December the 3rd an agreement is finally reached. On December the 3rd the White House notifies the Homeland Security Committee via email that they support the negotiated text that does not allow visa waivers for specific groups or categories. Okay? That is December 3rd.

December 3rd at 10:37 in the morning, White House notifies CHS, Committee on Homeland Security staff, that the State Department has no further edits to that text. Okay? President signed H.R. 2029 into law, which included the Visa Waiver Program language.

December the 19th Secretary Kerry sends a letter to the Iranian Foreign Minister stating that the U.S. will implement the requirements of this law so as not to interfere with the legitimate business interests of Iran. He ought to be talking about the legitimate business interests and the national security interests of the nation of the United States of America, but that is what he said.

Then on January the 21st Homeland Security announced implementation plans for the Visa Waiver Program enhancements with five broad categories of waivers, including category exemptions that were rejected, specifically rejected during the negotiations by Congress through December the 2nd.

Are you familiar, sir, Ambassador, with the Visa Waiver recommendation paper memo, white paper issued by the State Department?

Ambassador MULL. I have seen many papers that were involved in discussion of deciding what the administration's policy would be in implementing case by case waivers. I——

Mr. DUNCAN. Well let me, let me, I will remind the committee and you that during the negotiations the Congress and the administration, including the State Department said they agreed with the text and the negotiated text through the passage of the Omnibus. And then shortly thereafter they issued this white paper which talks about, it actually references a second white paper called a legal paper within this document. I have no idea what that is and we don't have our hands on that yet.

But in this paper it specifically comes up with a rationale for circumventing the will of Congress, as well outlined during the negotiations, during the Omnibus and during the Visa Waiver Program law, signed by the President. Before the ink is even dry on that bill, they are issuing a white paper on how to circumvent that with rationale.

I think it points to actually negotiating in bad faith in December before an Omnibus if the State Department feels like they are going to go around the will of Congress, to go around these negotiations and actually allow the issue of waivers, visa waivers for people that have traveled to Iran from European countries.

To the simple point that part of it says this is one of the questions they are going to ask, Madam Chairman, for someone traveling on business purposes. Simple question: Was your travel to Iraq—and this was the Iraq portion but I think it applies to Iran as well—after March 1st, 2011? If yes, was the travel exclusively for business purposes?

It is a pretty benign question to be asking. I mean there is not a lot of opportunity for delving into what the business was related to, who they were talking with. And going back to Mr. Sherman's comments, as the negotiation—I mean the conversation with Mr. Smith went on a minute ago about contact with IRGC. We are talking about European businesses, not American businesses, European businesses and business men and women that are traveling to Iran, who may have contact with Iran Revolutionary Guard, Quds Force, whoever, possibly come back to their home country in Europe and apply for travel to the United States under the Visa Waiver Program. And according to the State Department, they are going to be given a waiver.

That goes against the will of the Congress, sir. We are going to delve into this more, Madam Chairman. I wanted to say, Mr. Chairman, I wanted to say all this on the record. And I would ask that this document be submitted for the record for my colleagues on both sides of the aisle to delve into this a little further.

And with that I yield back.

Chairman ROYCE [presiding]. Without objection.

We go now to Lois Frankel from Florida.

Ms. FRANKEL. Thank you, Mr. Chair. Thank you, Ranking Member for this hearing. And thank you, gentlemen, for being here.

I have two sort of, I think they are sort of related questions. First has to do with the snapping back the sanctions. You know, we have read about a lot of economic activity now with Iran, with other countries. So my first question is, realistically, let us say we look 2 years ahead from now or 3 years ahead from now and we had to do a snap-back, what is the prospect of actually, actually getting back to where we were before we lifted the sanctions?

That is the first question.

Second question I have is that, you know, we hear talk of people—I am not going to get political—but there have been Presidential candidates who have said, Well, if I get elected I am going to immediately rip up the deal. And I would like to know what you think the implications of that, of that would be?

Those are my two questions. Thank you.

Ambassador MULL. Thank you very much, Congresswoman.

In terms of a snap-back, if we get to a situation in which Iran is not complying with the agreement and we decide to snap back those sanctions, reimposing the secondary sanctions, as my colleague Mr. Smith mentioned earlier, we have been down this road before where our European or other partners have an economic relationship with Iran, companies from those countries do. But for whatever reason we decided to penalize and to force those countries and companies to make the choice: Either you do business with Iran or you do business with us.

Every single time they choose to do business with us because it is a more profitable relationship. So I have no doubt that if we decided to snap back sanctions, that we would be effective in achieving that.

In terms of various interests, as some candidates have said, that they might rip up the deal on a first day in office of a new presidency, I would only say that I would advise whoever the new President and his or her team would be upon taking office, that to think very carefully about destroying a deal if Iran has continued to comply, which has reduced its breakout time, extended it from one, 1 or 2 months, to over a year. Iran has drastically shrunk the amount of enriched nuclear material that could lead to a bomb.

I am not, I am not sure I see what the benefit to U.S. interests would be in freeing Iran from those commitments that have made our interests much safer.

Ms. FRANKEL. Mr. Smith, did you want to answer?

Mr. SMITH. I would just agree with what Ambassador Mull said with respect to sanctions snap-back. The world knows what we can do with our secondary sanctions, and I think they will follow.

We are all very trained in what the secondary sanctions can accomplish. And they know the force of U.S. law in this area.

Ms. FRANKEL. But I guess would it be safe, though, to—I don't know if the word ''safe'' is correct—but I would assume that even if you put the sanctions back in place immediately, you are still not going to—it is still going to take a while for Iran to actually feel the same impact that they felt before they went to the table.

Mr. SMITH. It may take some time before Iran feels sanctions if they come back on. But we should remember where we are today. Iran is in a $½-trillion hole because of the sanctions that we have imposed over the course of time. Now they are facing a drop in oil prices just as the sanctions relief is coming into play.

What we are talking about is them getting about $50 billion, much of which they need desperately to prop up their currency, to be able to do any foreign trade. So when you look at the $50 billion that is relieved that they are getting versus the $½-trillion they have, I think it is going to be a very long time before Iran gets out from under the sanctions burden that we have imposed.

Ms. FRANKEL. Thank you.

I yield back, Mr. Chair.

Chairman ROYCE. We go now to Mr. Perry of Pennsylvania.

Mr. PERRY. Thank you, Mr. Chairman. Thank you, gentlemen for being here.

I will tell you that I appreciated the very direct questioning of Mr. Connolly and the very direct answers on very specific items. But I would also tell you that in my view, Iran has played long ball and we have played—we have been myopic. And while this, I think it has been early to talk about cheating on some of the specifics, but I do think in time that they will get there.

And but I just see them as consolidating their gains in Syria and Yemen and Iraq, and then using their ballistic technology, completing that testing in that program over a series of years to the point where when they are ready to be nuclear there will be very little that we can do with it. And that is the long ball and that is the long goal. I see Iran as the regional hegemon.

But in that, within that context let me ask you, Ambassador, a question here. The procurement channel in the United Nations Security Council 2231 allow for nuclear articles and dual-use articles to be provided to Iran from foreign suppliers through a dedicated procurement channel. However, some of the materials on dual-use list that can be supplied through the dedicated procurement channel are critical for Iran's ballistic missile program, such as carbon fiber. I know you are aware.

So this is a simple yes or no question: Would Iran's acquisition of carbon fiber outside of the dedicated procurement channel so in here described be a violation of the agreement and/or the U.N. Security Council resolution?

Ambassador MULL. Congressman Perry, I am sorry I can't give a yes or no answer because each case would be dependent on what exactly the intended use of any such materials through that channel would be.

The United States has a veto in the procurement channel. And so any time that we believe that an item is going to improve Iran's ballistic missile program or is going to be delivered in a way that is not subject to appropriate end use monitoring, I can't imagine the circumstances in which the United States would agree to a case like that.

Mr. PERRY. Let me make sure I understand your answer. You said it would be episodic; right? It depends on the, because of the dual-use proposition. But then you kind of said, I think, that the United States, understanding and recognizing that, wouldn't be amenable to their procurement of that. Is that? Did I characterize that correctly or not?

Ambassador MULL. Well, again, we would examine what is the good that they are seeking to procure, what is the stated purpose of its use, will it be monitored in a way that we are satisfied that it won't be used in a way to harm our interests across whatever.

Mr. PERRY. I mean you know that they can't domestically produce carbon fiber; right?

Ambassador MULL. As of now, yes.

Mr. PERRY. And you know it is critical for their ballistic missile program, I am sure.

And it is regulated through the procurement channel. So how would it not be monitored if it is regulated through the procurement? How would its use not be monitored?

Ambassador MULL. Well, according to the terms of implementation of the procurement channel, any country that wants to sell any material that is subject to controls of the procurement channel, as part of their applying for permission to proceed with the transaction they must explain how they are planning to monitor the end, the end use.

I would also add that we have a number of other tools outside of the procurement channel such as the missile technology control regime that we will continue to——

Mr. PERRY. I don't mean to interrupt but I have a limited amount of time.

Ambassador MULL. Yes.

Mr. PERRY. So Rouhani has already stated that it is their intention to expand their ballistic missile program and that they will have to gain access to carbon fiber elsewhere, and it will not go through the procurement channel. Are you familiar with that, that he said that?

Ambassador MULL. I am familiar in broad terms with what he said about how he plans to develop the missile program, yes.

Mr. PERRY. So if or when they do buy outside the procurement channel, which then there is no—because it is outside you don't know what they are using it for and there is no inspection paradigm or verification paradigm associated with that, would the administration consider that a violation of the agreement and the Security Council resolution?

Ambassador MULL. So, Congressman, the, I mean what is subject to the control of the procurement channel is a very specific list of nuclear suppliers with annexes of potential dual-use material and other essentially controlled nuclear-related items.

Mr. PERRY. Including carbon fiber?

Ambassador MULL. Well, it depends. It depends what exactly is the use.

Mr. PERRY. What does it depend on?

Ambassador MULL. What it would be——

Mr. PERRY. They are going to go outside the procurement channel, as stated by Rouhani.

Ambassador MULL. Sir, I can assure you that we will use every technique at our, and every tool at our disposal——

Mr. PERRY. Including considering it a violation——

Ambassador MULL [continuing]. Whether it is——

Mr. PERRY. Including considering it a violation? Yes or no?

Ambassador MULL. Well, a violation would be if Iran procures something on the nuclear suppliers' group list of annexes outside of the procurement channel.

Mr. PERRY. Including carbon fiber. So the answer would be ''yes.''
With your indulgence, Mr. Chairman.

Ambassador MULL. Yes. Yes, sir, carbon fiber.

Mr. PERRY. Okay, thank you. I appreciate your time.

45

Mr. Chairman, I yield.

Chairman ROYCE. Thank you, Mr. Perry.

We now go to Mr. Alan Lowenthal of California.

Mr. LOWENTHAL. Thank you, Mr. Chair. And thank you, Ambassador Mull and Mr. Smith for being so forthright in answering questions.

I want to follow up on some of the questions that Mr. Connolly has addressed. And I think this is really to you, Ambassador Mull. And you have already, I think, described to us about the removal of the core of the plutonium reactor. You have already described to us about the shutting down of the thousands of centrifuges, the shipping out of the country of its highly enriched uranium in exchange for lower level nuclear fuel for its nuclear power plants. I am going to follow up on these questions.

And I am curious about the extraction of that highly enriched uranium stockpile. If you can tell us how that was done; it was sent out of the country? Where it was taken? What steps we are taking to ensure that it is a permanent transfer and that the Iranian regime will not be able to get its hands on that or other highly enriched uranium in the future?

Ambassador MULL. Yes, sir. Thank you, Congressman Lowenthal.

Iran agreed that it would remove virtually all of its enriched nuclear material.

Mr. LOWENTHAL. Right.

Ambassador MULL. To keep that obligation, what it decided to do was to negotiate with Russia the transfer of that material out of Iran on a Russian ship into Russian custody, without any claim of title to that information. So it has surrendered this material to Russia.

Russia has committed to responsibly safeguard it within the side, within its entire nuclear program that it has there, a long history obviously, of maintaining and safeguarding nuclear materials.

Mr. LOWENTHAL. Are we able to know, is there some way that we can follow up on that? Or will we be monitoring and where the Russ—both the Russians and Iranians are, so that that enriched plutonium does never return back to Iran?

Ambassador MULL. Yes, sir. I mean we worked with the IAEA through this agreement to make sure that any possible entry point of nuclear material like that back into Iran could only take place under the observation and monitoring of the IAEA. So if there were some development by which someone tried to do that, we would be aware of it, and we would consider that a violation.

Mr. LOWENTHAL. And approximately how much was delivered to Russia?

Ambassador MULL. About 25,000 pounds of enriched uranium material.

Mr. LOWENTHAL. And what could 25,000 pounds of enriched uranium do? How much, how much would it take to—of that to develop nuclear weapons?

Ambassador MULL. None of that material. The highest grade of enrichment of that material that was removed was at 19.75 percent. Nuclear weapons material, weapons grade uranium really has to be at the 90 percent level or higher, highly enriched uranium.

Mr. LOWENTHAL. I am going to follow up. You know, a lot of us voted, and I was proud to support the agreement, but we had concerns about the implementation. So that is why we are so glad that the two of you are here today. And we are concerned, as some of these questions have been raised, about Iran's other non-nuclear trouble making, the security of Israel in the region. These are all concerns. The Congress wants to stay abreast of the compliance and any violations.

You know, in the letter in August to my colleagues from New York, Congressmember—to New York Congressmember Mr. Nadler, the President allayed many of these concerns and he detailed his plan, which included committing a highly qualified senior official with Ambassador rank to monitor them. That is really your position now that has come up.

What I am interested in is in your role do you have all the proper access and information that you are going to need? Are there any things that you are going to need to regularly report? And how often can we expect those kinds of interactions with you to follow up on this?

Ambassador MULL. Yes, sir. I am at your disposal and at the disposal of any Member of Congress to come down here any time and answer any questions or concerns that you have. I feel extraordinarily well supported by the entire administration. I have regular, rich, frequent interactions with various representatives of our intelligence community. I have access regularly to Secretary Kerry, other senior officials in the White House, who are very much focused on the implementation of this deal.

So I feel very well supported. And I am, and my team and I are——

Mr. LOWENTHAL. So you understand this is just a first, we have just begun this process, and that you are—will be very much agreeable to be coming back to the committee to reporting on a regular, because I think it is critically important that we stay in touch.

Ambassador MULL. Yes. Absolutely, sir, I think this is a vitally important part of my job because you may raise questions that I haven't thought of. And this is about the interests of all of our country. So I very much want to be a good partner for the committee.

Mr. LOWENTHAL. Well, I will be calling upon you.

Ambassador MULL. I look forward to it.

Mr. LOWENTHAL. Thank you. And I yield back.

Chairman ROYCE. Thank you, Mr. Lowenthal.

Now we go to Mr. Mark Meadows from North Carolina.

Mr. MEADOWS. Thank you, Mr. Chairman.

Mr. Smith, let me come to you with regards you are talking about this trillion-dollar hole, that the sanctions have had great effect. So let me just maybe narrow our focus a bit as it relates to Hezbollah and the financing of Hezbollah.

I guess I know that you implemented some of these sanctions in January, the announcement of the sanctions. But my question, I guess, goes really to the heart of the matter and it is with regards to Iran and are they financing Hezbollah in your professional opinion?

Mr. SMITH. I think we have seen Iran support Hezbollah over time, yes.

Mr. MEADOWS. Are they today?

Mr. SMITH. I haven't seen the latest figure. But I would——

Mr. MEADOWS. Well, within the last 6 months wouldn't you agree——

Mr. SMITH. We have seen Iran continue to support Hezbollah.

Mr. MEADOWS. So at what point would you consider putting sanctions on Iran, whether it is through the executive order that is in place or through the new law that the President just signed into law in December, at what point will you consider putting sanctions on Iran for supporting Hezbollah?

Mr. SMITH. So Iran is already under a government blocking from here. We——

Mr. MEADOWS. I am talking about, listen, I understand it. I am talking about the additional tools that you have, at what point will you implement additional sanctions as it relates to Hezbollah and the financing that comes from Iran?

Mr. SMITH. I will have to look at the evidence in the future and see where it takes us. That is what we do, we follow the evidence, and when we see evidence we continue to develop targets to add them to our list.

Mr. MEADOWS. Well, but your testimony is is that the last intelligence you had was that they are financing Hezbollah. Let's be intellectually honest. I think we both know that they are. Is it not true that the greatest benefactor of Iran's support, or the greatest benefactor for Hezbollah is Iran?

Mr. SMITH. That is a statistic that I am not sure that I have. I don't want to go beyond what I can tell you.

Mr. MEADOWS. Can you give it to this committee and to the chairman?

Mr. SMITH. I think we could get that to you in perhaps another setting, a classified setting.

Mr. MEADOWS. All right. So then under your professional opinion, who might be a greater financier of Hezbollah other than perhaps their illegal drug activities? What other state sponsor could be greater than Iran?

Mr. SMITH. Sir, I have already acknowledged that I think that Iran has continued to do so. I just, I don't want to go beyond my answer.

Mr. MEADOWS. The American people see pictures of sailors on an anniversary today and they are offended. I am offended. And if we have tools in place that can address it and you are not using them, would you not believe that that is being irresponsible?

Mr. SMITH. Sir, we are continuing to use our tools. We are continuing to designate. Virtually every month, every week we are adding additional designations of terrorists. We did so yesterday. I think we will continue to do so in the very near future to oppose terrorism.

Mr. MEADOWS. But the big black hole here, Mr. Smith, is Iran. We are going all around it. We have got over 100 individuals—and I agree with you, I have been following the numbers—we are addressing it. But somehow Iran is getting a free pass. And that is concerning to the American people.

Mr. SMITH. I would disagree with you about Iran getting a free pass. There are a number of agencies of the Government of Iran that continue to be designated by the United States for their support to terrorism, a number of significant individuals that continue to be designated of the Government of Iran for their support to terrorism. And those carry secondary sanctions consequences.

Mr. MEADOWS. Ambassador Mull, let me come to you and follow up on a question that actually came up yesterday. Some of your colleagues behind you were there in a hearing at OGR as it related to the Visa Waiver Program. Mr. Duncan of South Carolina mentioned that. Under what, since you are responsible for making sure that this JCPOA stays in place, was there language in there that would allow Iran to actually participate in our Visa Waiver Program, either directly or indirectly? Because they are participating indirectly now. Was there language in there that would suggest that they should enjoy those benefits?

Ambassador MULL. Language in the, I am sorry, in the legislation or in the——

Mr. MEADOWS. Well, we know there was in our language.

Ambassador MULL. Not in the legislation, sir.

Mr. MEADOWS. In the joint agreement. Because Secretary Kerry came out and——

Ambassador MULL. Yes. Yes.

Mr. MEADOWS [continuing]. Very quickly said that we are going to expand it to business-related activities——

Ambassador MULL. Right.

Mr. MEADOWS [continuing]. Which was not——

Ambassador MULL. Yes. So, Congressman, thank you very much for the opportunity. I would like to address, I think this is a critical misunderstanding that I really welcome the opportunity to clarify.

The JCPOA, in that agreement all of the parties agreed that they would not attempt to block legitimate business activity in Iran. When this legislation was passed, the Iranians immediately complained to me, to Secretary Kerry, accusing us of violating the JCPOA through this legislation.

That is decidedly not the case. We explained to them that this legislation was not aimed at disrupting Iran's business activity, it was aimed at protecting America's borders. And it was in that context that Secretary Kerry in fact defended the legislation responding to this untrue charge that the Iranians had leveled.

Mr. MEADOWS. I yield back. Thank you, Mr. Chairman.

Chairman ROYCE. Okay, we are going to go with Mr. William Keating of Massachusetts.

Mr. KEATING. Thank you, Mr. Chairman. I want to thank our witnesses for being here today and thank you for your direct answers to questions.

There is one area I just have left because we have covered so much ground as a committee here this morning, and that is, those are the issues for violations outside the JCPOA that we were told during the whole process will be vigorously, you know, pursued. We talked about some of the areas this morning where that would be relevant, including support of terrorism, regional destabilization, human rights abuses, and ballistic missile programs.

And we do know that Iran tested a precision-guided ballistic missile capable of delivering a nuclear warhead, in violation of U.N. agreements. We are aware that the U.S. sanctioned 11 individuals and entities responsible for supporting these kind of activities.

Now, my question is this in terms of your oversight, in terms of our ability as a committee to work with you and communicate in monitoring this. And I know you can't be very specific on this because of your leverage is sanctions in the future.

But in these sanctions outside the JCPOA, can you just shed a little light on how you work administratively with other agencies of our Government? Can you just shed some light on the process where you are determining what you give for sanctions at a certain level, what factors are going to result in your reviewing that and changing those sanctions, maybe escalating them, whether it is continued violations, whether it is continuing—How, how do you arrive at that?

How is that, how do you function administratively in reviewing those, setting those, so that we have a better sense going forward on these very important sanctions that are outside the agreement?

Mr. SMITH. Thank you, sir. I think that is a very important question. I am happy to try to shed some light on it.

As I sit here today, we have teams of analysts at the Treasury Department who are pouring through the intelligence and other information that we have from a variety of sources. The intelligence community, from the Defense Department, from all of the agencies of the U.S. Government, they look at the classified and unclassified information that is available and they focus on the different sanctions programs that we have.

So I have a team that is working on terrorism, Hezbollah sanctions, ISIL sanctions, everything in the terrorism realm, whether it is Iran-related or not Iran-related, we follow the intel.

We also have teams working on our Syria sanctions, including any support to Syria, as well as anything dealing with Yemen, destabilizing activities in the region, and also teams that focus on the ballistic missile program. We gather the evidence to see if we see anything that fits within the sanctions program. And then, if we do, we start to develop a case on it. We talk to the rest of the interagency so everybody is on board so they know what we are doing.

We don't want to, for example, interrupt a sensitive intelligence operation. We don't want to interfere with a law enforcement operation. So we make sure that what we do we communicate very well, so that when we roll out we are able to roll out in the smartest, most effective way.

So basically we start form scratch developing the intel, building cases, working with the team so that we can roll out successive sanctions against the greatest threats for our national security and foreign policy.

Mr. KEATING. Yes. And in that process, what triggers reevaluating things? Without getting into detail, because I don't want to undercut the leverage you have, but I mean what are the things that are important that you are looking at and you say, you know, they are not reacting to these sanctions, we are going to have to leverage this up? What kind of things are you looking at?

Mr. SMITH. I think we, we continue to look at our experience across all of our sanctions programs. We have a good idea of what is impactful. And that is why when we wanted to have an impact on Iran in many of these other sanctions programs, for ballistic missiles there are major entities that do the ballistic missile program: SHIG, and SBIG, and MODAFL, and all of the big names in Iran that are associated with the ballistic missile program, we hit those. And then we go after anyone outside of Iran that we see supporting that program.

So that is why last month we went after a UAE- and China-based network that we saw that was supporting that program. So, again, we follow the evidence to see what is going to have an impact. And the evidence sometimes will suggest different impacts for different programs. And so we try to get the networks that are most critical to those bad activities.

Mr. KEATING. So it is a dynamic situation, it is not, you know, something which, that is incremental. Here we go, we are going to impose this now. Let's see, it is continually being evaluated; is that correct?

Mr. SMITH. Those under sanctions know how to try to circumvent them. And so we have to continue to evolve.

Mr. KEATING. Well, thank you. That will help us as we go forward. Because this committee is certainly going to be concerned on these other violations going forward and how the U.S. reacts. And this will help give us our ability to perform the oversight function more properly.

So thank you very much. I yield back.

Chairman ROYCE. Thank you very much, Mr. Keating.

We go to Ted Yoho of Florida.

Mr. YOHO. Thank you, Mr. Chairman. Gentlemen, I appreciate you being here.

In your opinion, I think we already know the question or answer to this, Hezbollah they are, we could assume they are a terrorist organization that carries out proxy work for Iran? Agreed?

Mr. SMITH. Yes.

Mr. YOHO. With Iran offering to put GPS technology on 100,000 missiles, would we assume that is for peaceful purposes or terrorist purposes?

Mr. SMITH. I will just say Iran's development of its ballistic missile program is something that remains under sanction by the U.S. Government, and we continue to go after it.

Mr. YOHO. Okay, good.

So if they are supporting Hezbollah and giving this kind of technology to over 100,000 missiles, we can assume that is probably not for good reasons; right? I mean——

Mr. SMITH. I am going to continue to follow the evidence. And——

Mr. YOHO. Well, the evidence points that it is going there. And, you know, if it walks like a duck, quacks like a duck, it is a duck. This is, this is not a good thing.

And that brings me to the opening remarks of the chairman. President Obama in the Rose Garden pledged to remain vigilant and respond to Iran's continued sponsorship of terrorism, its support for proxies who destabilize the Middle East, and threats against American friends and allies.

Iran's destabilizing activity has continued in the wake of the nuclear deal. Is that not breaching the JCPOA?

Ambassador MULL. Sir, the JCPOA is exclusively focused on Iran's nuclear program.

Mr. YOHO. I want to take you to measure 28 of the JCPOA which clearly states that "Iran and the E3/EU+3 will commit to implementing the JCPOA in good faith."

If they are doing terrorist activity, is that in good faith?

Ambassador MULL. Terrorism is outside the scope of the JCPOA.

Mr. YOHO. What about the development of ballistic missiles and the firing of those, are they outside of that?

Ambassador MULL. Yes, sir.

Mr. YOHO. What about breaching U.N. Security Resolutions 1929 or 2231, are they outside of the JCPOA agreement?

Ambassador MULL. Yes, sir. We deal with those problems in other avenues.

Mr. YOHO. All right. But also, "in good faith," that is a part of the JCPOA. In good faith and constructive atmosphere, based on mutual respect, and refraining from any action inconsistent with the letter, spirit, intent of the JCPOA that would undermine its successful implementation.

I mean we can argue which side of arming Hezbollah with 100,000 GPS-guided missiles, or firing medium range ballistic missiles as they did on November 22nd, I think it was, or November 20th, and then again on October 10th, which was before the agreement went into place.

The point I want to bring out here, it is pretty clear the intention of Iran is not to play, you know, abide by the JCPOA. What they are doing, they are taunting. And for the administration to release sanctions, I have a letter here that we wrote that has over 100 U.S. representatives that asked the President to hold off on sanctions. This was sent December 17th of 2015 by over 100 members of this body, Republicans and Democrats, that asked the President to look into this before we moved further. And there was no response from the President.

And I think this is a travesty to our negotiating. And I think it has weakened us. As we negotiate, I would only hope that our Government as we negotiate is from a position of strength that makes our country stronger.

Do you feel that this has made our country stronger, this negotiation, and what we have seen the actions of Iran do with the firing of these missiles, the firing of the missiles real close to our Navy destroyer, the way they apprehended our military personnel. And they make fun of them on the world scene. I mean do you think that has made our country stronger?

Ambassador MULL. No. That activity was outrageous. I am disgusted by those things.

Mr. YOHO. Okay. All right. So it has not made our country stronger.

Do you think the Iran nuclear deal has made Iran stronger?

Ambassador MULL. I believe it has constrained Iran's ability to develop a nuclear weapon and has made us safer as a result.

Mr. YOHO. What about bringing up their money? You know, Mr. Smith, you were talking about the $50 million or the 500, $½ trillion they are in debt. If a country is a $½ trillion in debt and they are screaming for economic release and relief, would you think a country that is in that dire straits and suffering that bad would be funding terrorist activity?

Mr. SMITH. Iran had continued to fund terrorist activities during the course of the sanctions programs——

Mr. YOHO. So how bad were they suffering? You know, I heard that through the JCPOA agreement and I didn't buy it. I didn't buy it then and I don't buy it now. And I hope what Mr. Duncan said does not come to fruition. It will either be a Neville Chamberlain moment or we can look back and say, you know what, that was a Ronald Reagan moment. And I hope it goes the right way.

I yield back. Thank you.

Chairman ROYCE. Thank you very much, Mr. Yoho.

We now go to Grace Meng of New York.

Ms. MENG. Thank you, Mr. Chairman. And thank you to Ambassador Mull and Mr. Smith for being here and all your hard work.

Since the JCPOA went into effect, Iran's hardliners have taken pains to consolidate their economic and political power and to sideline would-be reformists who are more amenable to a rapprochement with the West. It was hoped that the openings created by the JCPOA would engender Iranian moderation but, instead, extremists have reaped the benefits while tightening their grip and escalating their malign behavior.

Does the U.S. have a strategy to combat the retrenchment we see on the part of Khomeini, his allies, and the IRGC?

I will just go through all my questions in the interest of time.

How have Iran's terrorist activities been affected by the JCPOA? I know that you mentioned that it was outside the scope of the deal, but what do you know about if their support for terrorism has increased or decreased?

Does the U.S. have an estimate of the amount of funding that Iran provides to groups like Hezbollah? How are the funds being transferred?

And if we see an Iranian bank transfer of funds for the benefit of groups like Hezbollah, will the U.S. immediately sanction that bank?

And if we are to go beyond sanctions, is the administration pursuing any actions beyond sanctions to confront any of Iran's problematic behavior in the region? And, if so, what are these actions?

Ambassador MULL. Thank you very much, Congresswoman. In terms of the impact of the JCPOA in the internal Iranian political situation, you are right, many people have expressed various views and hopes and aspirations and the impact that it would have. But the principal reason for the administration to pursue this has really been to diminish Iran's ability to build a nuclear weapon. And in that so far we have exceeded demonstrably by increasing Iran's breakout time to at least a year.

So it wouldn't be appropriate for me to speculate. We are not really implementing this deal to have a political impact on Iran. It is all about protecting us from a nuclear Iran. And as I said, in that we have succeeded.

In terms of penalizing Iran's destabilizing activity in the region, we have a rich set of tools that we can use. And we, as Mr. Smith has been describing, and I will let him address in more detail, we have shown a readiness to do that. We have penalized, most recently on January 17th, Iran's missile, ballistic missile program. In the past few weeks we have continued to sanction Hezbollah activities and people linked to Hezbollah. And we will continue to do that at this point.

Mr. SMITH. I would just add and say, Congresswoman, I don't have the exact amount that Iran uses to fund terrorism. We can go back and see. I think the intelligence community probably has the best number working with the Treasury Department. But that would be more of a classified figure that we would have to provide in a different setting.

In terms of sanctioning Iranian banks for bad behavior in support of terrorism, we have done it. We have sanctioned Bank Saderat in the past for its support for terrorism. We will continue to follow the evidence of support for terrorism, ballistic missile support, destabilizing activities. And we will develop packages and targets when we see the evidence.

Ms. MENG. And finally, but can we tell if the support for terrorist activities and groups have increased or decreased and the amounts?

Ambassador MULL. Again, Congresswoman, I think Mr. Smith is right that I think we would be happy to go into more detail in a different setting. But I do note that General Clapper recently testified in the past few days that he has not seen an appreciable change in Iranian level of support since the implementation of this deal.

Ms. MENG. Okay.

Ambassador MULL. Support for terrorism.

Ms. MENG. Thank you. I yield back.

Chairman ROYCE. Thank you, Congresswoman Grace Meng.

Ambassador, Ranking Member Engel and I both mentioned Iran's horrible behavior in the neighborhood. And that includes Iranian-backed forces that threaten those at Camp Ashraf. The committee raised this with Ambassador McGurk yesterday.

And I pass these concerns on to you. These individuals need protection. The U.S. Government needs to guarantee that protection. And we have seen what has happened of late in terms of loss of human life there at the camp. So I would, I would convey to you what I conveyed to him yesterday, to the Ambassador yesterday, which is this needs to be a priority.

We appreciate the time of both of you as witnesses here today before the committee. You heard the deep concerns that many of our members have about Iran policy and how it is being carried out. So I know that you will want to continue to be in touch with members of this committee as we move forward.

And at this time we will adjourn the hearing. Thank you again for your appearance.

[Whereupon, at 12:15 p.m., the committee was adjourned.]

APPENDIX

FULL COMMITTEE HEARING NOTICE
COMMITTEE ON FOREIGN AFFAIRS
U.S. HOUSE OF REPRESENTATIVES
WASHINGTON, DC 20515-6128

Edward R. Royce (R-CA), Chairman

February 11, 2016

TO: MEMBERS OF THE COMMITTEE ON FOREIGN AFFAIRS

You are respectfully requested to attend an OPEN hearing of the Committee on Foreign Affairs, to be held in Room 2172 of the Rayburn House Office Building (and available live on the Committee website at http://www.ForeignAffairs.house.gov):

DATE: Thursday, February 11, 2016

TIME: 10:00 a.m.

SUBJECT: Iran Nuclear Deal Oversight: Implementation and its Consequences

WITNESSES: The Honorable Stephen D. Mull
Lead Coordinator for Iran Nuclear Implementation
U.S. Department of State

Mr. John Smith
Acting Director
Office of Foreign Assets Control
U.S. Department of the Treasury

By Direction of the Chairman

The Committee on Foreign Affairs seeks to make its facilities accessible to persons with disabilities. If you are in need of special accommodations, please call 202/225-5021 at least four business days in advance of the event, whenever practicable. Questions with regard to special accommodations in general (including availability of Committee materials in alternative formats and assistive listening devices) may be directed to the Committee.

COMMITTEE ON FOREIGN AFFAIRS
MINUTES OF FULL COMMITTEE HEARING

Day___*Thursday*____Date_____*2/11/2016*_____Room_____*2172*_____

Starting Time _____*10:04*_____Ending Time ___*12:15*_____

Recesses ___*0*___ (____to ____) (____to ____) (____to ____) (____to ____) (____to ____) (____to ____)

Presiding Member(s)

Chairman Edward R. Royce, Rep. Ileana Ros-Lehtinen, Rep. Chris Smith

Check all of the following that apply:

Open Session ☑   Electronically Recorded (taped) ☑
Executive (closed) Session ☐   Stenographic Record ☑
Televised ☑

TITLE OF HEARING:

Iran Nuclear Deal Oversight: Implementation and its Consequences

COMMITTEE MEMBERS PRESENT:

See attached.

NON-COMMITTEE MEMBERS PRESENT:

none

HEARING WITNESSES: Same as meeting notice attached? Yes ☑ No ☐
(If "no", please list below and include title, agency, department, or organization.)

STATEMENTS FOR THE RECORD: *(List any statements submitted for the record.)*

IFR - Rep. Jeff Duncan
SFR - Rep. Gerald Connolly
QFR - Rep. Michael McCaul

TIME SCHEDULED TO RECONVENE_____
or
TIME ADJOURNED *12:15*_____

Jean Marter, Director of Committee Operations

HOUSE COMMITTEE ON FOREIGN AFFAIRS
FULL COMMITTEE HEARING

PRESENT	MEMBER
X	Edward R. Royce, CA
X	Christopher H. Smith, NJ
X	Ileana Ros-Lehtinen, FL
X	Dana Rohrabacher, CA
X	Steve Chabot, OH
X	Joe Wilson, SC
	Michael T. McCaul, TX
X	Ted Poe, TX
X	Matt Salmon, AZ
	Darrell Issa, CA
X	Tom Marino, PA
X	Jeff Duncan, SC
X	Mo Brooks, AL
X	Paul Cook, CA
X	Randy Weber, TX
X	Scott Perry, PA
X	Ron DeSantis, FL
X	Mark Meadows, NC
X	Ted Yoho, FL
	Curt Clawson, FL
	Scott DesJarlais, TN
	Reid Ribble, WI
	Dave Trott, MI
X	Lee Zeldin, NY
X	Dan Donovan, NY

PRESENT	MEMBER
X	Eliot L. Engel, NY
X	Brad Sherman, CA
	Gregory W. Meeks, NY
	Albio Sires, NJ
X	Gerald E. Connolly, VA
X	Theodore E. Deutch, FL
	Brian Higgins, NY
X	Karen Bass, CA
X	William Keating, MA
X	David Cicilline, RI
	Alan Grayson, FL
X	Ami Bera, CA
X	Alan S. Lowenthal, CA
X	Grace Meng, NY
X	Lois Frankel, FL
X	Tulsi Gabbard, HI
	Joaquin Castro, TX
	Robin Kelly, IL
	Brendan Boyle, PA

MATERIAL SUBMITTED FOR THE RECORD BY THE HONORABLE JEFF DUNCAN, A
REPRESENTATIVE IN CONGRESS FROM THE STATE OF SOUTH CAROLINA

VWP Waiver Recommendation Paper

The Visa Waiver Program Improvement and Terrorist Travel Prevention Act of 2015, enacted as
part of the Consolidated Appropriations Act, 2016, amended the Immigration and Nationality
Act to make ineligible for participation in the Visa Waiver Program (VWP) any person who has
been present in Iran, Iraq, Sudan, or Syria since March 1, 2011, with two very limited exceptions
(travel to perform military services in a VWP country's armed forces and travel to carry out
official duties as an employee of a VWP government).

The law gives the Secretary of Homeland Security authority to waive this ineligibility if the
Secretary determines that such a waiver is in the law enforcement or national security interests of
the United States. As discussed in the legal paper, this is a lesser standard than that imposed by
other statutes that require a finding that a waiver is "vital to" or "essential to" the national
security interests of the United States. Furthermore, there are no findings of fact or other
determinations required to be made before exercise of the waiver authority. Additionally, as
discussed in the legal paper, the national security waiver can be exercised by category, not just
individuals.

State recommends waivers for the following classes of persons:

1. Business-related travel to Iran following the conclusion of the JCPOA (July 14, 2015).
Rationale: The VWP legislation and its implementation do not violate U.S. commitments
under the JCPOA. Nevertheless, these provisions do have the potential to cause citizens
of VWP countries to hesitate to travel to Iran for business, which could adversely affect
normalization of trade with Iran and, in turn, Iran's commitment to implementing the
JCPOA. Moreover, these provisions could adversely affect the strength of our partnership
with the EU and with non-EU states in addressing Iranian (and other) issues. Thus, it is
in the national security interest of the United States to waive the VWP ineligibility for
individuals who have traveled to Iran for legitimate business purposes after July 14,
2015, or will travel to Iran for legitimate business purposes in the future.

Iranian Dual nationals: This category should also include dual nationals of Iran who have
traveled to Iran for legitimate business purposes since that date. Including dual nationals
is appropriate for both of the national security reasons listed above, since these
individuals will be important facilitators for companies that want to trade with Iran.

Legal argument: This limited approach is directly tied to JCPOA implementation and
avoids burdening close allies whose nationals traveled to Iran for legitimate business
purposes after the deal was concluded. As discussed in the legal paper, this approach is
defensible based on the specific national security interests associated with maintaining
the strength of international partnerships, as well as JCPOA implementation. DHS, in
consultation with State, would have to determine what business travel would be viewed
as "legitimate" and hence covered by the waiver. A baseline would be travel to Iran for
business-related activities that were not prohibited or sanctionable under U.S. law and
regulations or pursuant to UNSC resolutions at the time when the travel occurred.

Specific ESTA language: Questions should be added to elicit whether individuals traveled to Iran for legitimate business purposes. Possible questions include: "Was your travel to Iran after July 14, 2015? If yes, was the travel for business purposes? If yes, please describe the travel, including the company or other entity for which you were traveling and all entities in Iran with which you had dealings." This last question would require some manual intervention by DHS to ensure the travel was for "legitimate business purposes," so State and DHS need to collaborate on the mechanics of such an approach. If it was considered important to elicit further information to validate the applicant's answers to these basic questions, additional questions that could be considered might include: For a dual national, whether the individual traveled with family members to Iran, as this could be an indicator that the purpose of travel was not solely business. Additionally, the travel question could ask, was the travel exclusively/solely for business purposes?

2. Employees of International and Regional Organizations and Sub-National Governments who traveled on official duty.

Rationale: The current law does not include an exemption from ineligibility for: employees of international organizations such as UN officials, IAEA inspectors, and employees of international humanitarian organizations; officials of the EU institutions or members of the European Parliament; sub-national parliaments of VWP countries; or similar bodies. It is in the national security interest of the United States to waive the VWP ineligibility for individuals who traveled to Iran, Iraq, Sudan or Syria on or after March 1, 2011, on official duties on behalf of one of these institutions.

Dual nationals: This category should also include dual nationals who are employees of one of these institutions, regardless of whether the individual has traveled to one of the four countries. Otherwise, we would undermine our national security interest in maintaining relationships with these institutions by placing restrictions on certain employees of these institutions.

Legal argument: As discussed in the legal paper, the United States has a national security interest in: (1) supporting engagement and other activities conducted by such institutions in each of these countries; and (2) maintaining strong relations and enhancing cooperation with those entities on a variety of objectives, including, among other things, counterterrorism, nonproliferation, and humanitarian assistance in conflict zones.

Specific ESTA language: The ESTA form could include a drop down question asking whether the individual traveled to one of the four countries for official duties as an employee of one of the following entities, with a list of specific institutions or categories of institutions to choose from.

3. Employees of Humanitarian Non-Governmental Organizations (NGO) who traveled on official duty.

Rationale: VWP country citizens who have worked for humanitarian NGOs in any of the four countries since March 2011 would be ineligible for the VWP.

Legal argument: It is in the national security interest of the United States to waive the VWP ineligibility for individuals who traveled to Iran, Iraq, Sudan or Syria on or after March 1, 2011 on official duties on behalf of non-governmental humanitarian organizations who, for example, provide humanitarian assistance in those countries. We could consider including employees of other NGOs that promote other specific objectives that are in the U.S. national security interest, such as NGOs from VWP countries doing work in Iran, Iraq, Sudan, and Syria that supports the U.S. national security interest in the advancement of civil society in repressive environments. Further, this restriction may have the consequence of making it more difficult for these organizations to recruit personnel from VWP countries, which would impact programs aimed at helping civilians in those countries.

Dual nationals: Since the national security interest is in the promotion of the work of these NGOs, this category should also include dual nationals who are employees of one of these NGOs, regardless of whether the individual has traveled to one of the four countries. Otherwise, we would undermine our national security interest by placing restrictions on certain employees in these organizations.

Specific ESTA language: The ESTA questions could include a drop down question asking whether the individual traveled to one of the four countries as an employee of such an NGO. A possible follow-up question would ask on behalf of which organization did the individual travel. Again, this may require some manual intervention by DHS regarding the legitimacy of the named NGOs.

4. Accredited Journalists who traveled for reporting purposes.

Rationale: The current law does not include an exemption from ineligibility for journalists, who are essential for understanding the situation in Iran, Iraq, Syria, and Sudan.

Legal argument: The United States has a national security interest in promoting the free flow of information regarding events and activities in Iran, Iraq, Sudan, and Syria. A waiver of the VWP ineligibility for accredited journalists who traveled to Iran, Iraq, Sudan or Syria on or after March 1, 2011, would help facilitate this national security interest of the United States.

Dual nationals: This category should include dual nationals who are accredited journalists and traveled to one of the four countries, especially in Iran. As a result, excluding this group could have a significant impact on the promotion of the free flow of information.

Specific ESTA language: The ESTA could include a drop down question asking whether the individual traveled to one of the four countries as an accredited journalist. A possible follow-up question would ask on behalf of which organization did the individual travel.

5. Dual-Nationals who emigrated from Iran in the aftermath of the Revolution.

Rationale: The current law excludes individuals who emigrated from Iran in the wake of the Revolution. This is a distinct group who merit special treatment.

Legal argument: The United States has a national security interest in Iran moderating politically over time. Penalizing those who emigrated from Iran in the aftermath of the Revolution runs counter to this objective because it alienates a group that largely support the United States goal of encouraging Iran to moderate politically.

Specific ESTA language: The ESTA could include a drop down question asking a dual-national from Iran, when he/she emigrated out of Iran. Further discussions are needed to assess the appropriate year for categorizing those who emigrated in the aftermath of Revolution.

6. Dual-Iranian nationals who were born outside of Iran.

Rationale: The current law excludes nationals of a VWP country who are also nationals of Iran, even if the Iranian nationality was acquired by operation of law, rather than an affirmative act by the individual.

Legal argument: The United States has a national security interest in Iran moderating politically over time. Penalizing those who were born outside of Iran runs counter to this objective because it alienates a group that largely support the U.S. goal of encouraging Iran to moderate politically.

Specific ESTA language: No additional language is needed.

7. Dual-Iranian nationals traveling to the United States for business purposes or as part of official duties as an employee of a Humanitarian Non-Governmental Organizations (NGO).

Rationale: The current law excludes nationals of a VWP country who are also nationals of Iran from traveling to the United States under the VWP. While this would be a broad category to include in a waiver, this group is engaged in activity that is important for the U.S. national security interest. Placing restrictions on humanitarian employees will make it harder for those organizations to recruit personnel from VWP countries, which would impact programs aimed at helping civilians in those countries.

Legal Argument: The United States has a national security interest in promoting business and humanitarian ties with our closest allies in VWP countries. The United States also has a national security interest in Iran moderating over time, and thus in not alienating those who largely support that U.S. goal. Placing restrictions on dual nationals from Iran engaging in these activities will undermine that interest.

Specific ESTA language: ESTA questions would need to be updated to seek the purpose of the travel to understand whether it was solely for business purposes or as an employee of a humanitarian NGO on official duties.

8. Business-related travel to Iraq

Rationale: We have a national security interest in ensuring the political stability of Iraq and enabling the government to effectively counter ISIL. One of the best ways to achieve these goals is to support the country's weak economy, which is overly dependent on declining oil revenue and is a threat to Prime Minister Abadi's ability to govern. That is why the U.S. has spent years trying to encourage international investment in Iraq, not only in oil infrastructure, but also in diversifying the economy to increase its resilience. The current law would undermine these efforts and our national security interests by placing restrictions on citizens of VWP countries who traveled to Iraq for business and engaged in key commercial activities that support the Iraqi government's revenue generation and directly affect Baghdad's ability to fund its fight against ISIL.

Legal argument: This approach is defensible based on the specific national security interests associated with maintaining the stability of Iraq and enabling the government to focus on countering ISIL.

Specific ESTA language: Questions should be added to elicit whether individuals traveled to Iraq for business purposes. Possible questions include: "Was your travel to Iraq after March 1, 2011? If yes, was the travel exclusively for business purposes?

Statement for the Record
Submitted by Mr. Connolly of Virginia

On January 16, 2016, Iran, the U.S., the European Union, and our P5+1 partners completed the requirements for implementing the Joint Comprehensive Plan of Action (JCPOA). The actions taken to reach this milestone were significant and on a scale that only concerted international diplomacy and pressure could achieve.

The International Atomic Energy Agency (IAEA) has certified that Iran significantly modified the Arak Heavy Water Research Reactor and that the reactor is no longer producing plutonium. Iran reduced its number of installed centrifuges from 19,000 to 6,104 at the fuel enrichment plants at Natanz and Fordow. Iran is no longer enriching uranium above 3.67% and has reduced its stockpile to no more than 300 kg. Centrifuge production and uranium mines and mills are under constant surveillance. Additionally, Iran has implemented the monitoring regimes of the Additional Protocol – which gives the IAEA expedient access to any site suspected of contributing to an illicit nuclear program – and Modified Code 3.1 – which requires advanced notice of any construction or design changes at a nuclear facility. The entire Iranian nuclear supply chain is now restricted and subject to monitoring by the IAEA.

As a matter of perspective, consider that prior to January 20, 2014 – implementation day for the Joint Plan of Action – Iran possessed an opaque and unconstrained nuclear program that had expanded from a negligible number of installed centrifuges to more than 19,000 in less than ten years. We were very quickly approaching a moment in which our only choice for arresting Iran's nuclear advance was a military operation.

That is no longer the imperative, and we should take every necessary precaution to sustain this welcome alternative – one in which the U.S. is the leader of an international coalition of countries who have coalesced around a shared goal of preventing Iran's development of a nuclear weapon.

Congress should work in concert with the Administration to ensure that the Iran nuclear deal is fully implemented and strictly enforced. To this end, I have introduced bipartisan legislation to establish a Congressional-Executive Commission to oversee the implementation of the JCPOA and verify Iran's compliance with its obligations under the deal. The Commission to Verify Iranian Compliance Act (H.R. 3741) will ensure close and enduring Congressional oversight of the JCPOA as well as coordination between Congress and the Administration regarding implementation of the deal.

The Commission will include 16 Members of Congress (8 from the Senate and 8 from the House of Representatives) and 4 representatives from the Executive Branch (representing the

Department of State, Department of Defense, Department of the Treasury, and Department of Energy). Commissioners will be appointed by the respective Chamber leadership, the leadership of the Senate Foreign Relations Committee and House Foreign Affairs Committee, and the President.

The Commission to Verify Iranian Nuclear Compliance is modeled after the Commission on Security and Cooperation in Europe, also known as the Helsinki Commission, which was created in 1976 to monitor compliance with the Helsinki Final Act. Despite initial pushback from the Nixon Administration, the Helsinki Commission has served as an oversight model and is still actively carrying out its mission nearly 40 years after it was established.

The JCPOA is a viable alternative for addressing the Iranian nuclear threat, and Congress should not be distracted by efforts to unilaterally reject a deal that has already been approved and implemented by the U.S. and our negotiating partners. It should instead look to bolster mechanisms for strict enforcement such as robust funding for the accounts that support the IAEA, the international organization tasked with implementing the JCPOA and other non-proliferation agreements.

Undermining the deal is not productive and efforts to do so expose that the opposition to this accord does not have a viable alternative to keeping the U.S. and our allies safe from the Iranian nuclear threat. The JCPOA is such an option, and we should support its implementation.

Questions for the Record Submitted to
Ambassador Stephen Mull
Representative McCaul
House Foreign Affairs Committee
February 11, 2016

Question:
Does this Administration want to encourage Iran to become more politically moderate over time? If so, then why are we enriching the one entity, the IRGC, which has been tasked with making sure that does not happen?

Answer:
The Islamic Revolutionary Guard Corps (IRGC) remains firmly under U.S. sanctions, which we have no intention of removing until the IRGC ceases the activities for which it has been sanctioned, including its support for terrorism. Executive Order (E.O.) 13224, which allows us to target terrorists of any stripe across the globe, is employed forcefully against Iran. The IRGC-Qods Force, the Iranian Ministry of Intelligence and Security, Iran's Mahan Air, Hizballah, and over 100 other Iran-related individuals and entities remain subject to sanctions under this E.O. Further, under Iran sanctions statutes, foreign financial institutions may be subject to secondary sanctions for knowingly facilitating a significant financial transaction or providing significant financial services for any entity on the SDN List, which includes the IRGC and IRGC-related officials, agents, and affiliates. These and other authorities allow us to continue to target the IRGC for any activities which threaten us or our allies.

Iran has a choice about how it moves forward. If Iran chooses to build on the constructive outcomes of the nuclear deal reached with the international community, it would lead to a better future for the Iranian people.

Question:
In determining whether to impose sanctions on Iran for violations of the JCPOA or for non-nuclear reasons, how do Iranian threats to abandon the JCPOA play into your considerations?

Answer:
We have always been clear that sanctions relief under the Joint Comprehensive Plan of Action (JCPOA) is contingent on Iran's fulfillment of its nuclear-related commitments. We are committed to ensuring that Iran fulfills all of its commitments in a verifiable and complete manner. Should Iran fail to fulfill its commitments, we retain a wide range of options to respond, including by re-imposing national and/or multilateral nuclear-related sanctions. Similarly, we have been clear that sanctions will remain an important tool to respond to Iran's other troubling activities, including its support for terrorism, human rights abuses, ballistic missile-related activities, and destabilizing activities in the region. If Iran used our imposition of sanctions in these areas as a pretext to stop performing its JCPOA commitments, such a decision would have enormous consequences for Iran, such as the re-imposition of the sanctions that have damaged its economy to date and isolation again from the international community.

Question:
As Iran becomes more entrenched in the international economy already having cut billion dollar deals with countries in Europe, will the idea of "snap back" sanctions become more and more difficult?

Answer:

The scenario you describe is the situation we were facing in 2012. Then, Iran seemed to be on the path towards a nuclear weapons capability and we won international agreement to impose very tough sanctions to cut off contracts and to pull out of investments. All of those costly steps were taken in 2012 because the world, frankly, does not want Iran to have that capability.

Under the Joint Comprehensive Plan of Action (JCPOA), if there is a significant violation by Iran, the United States has the ability to quickly re-impose the multilateral sanctions that were lifted. United Nations Security Council (UNSC) Resolution 2231 establishes an unprecedented mechanism under which we have the ability to re-impose UN sanctions on Iran – the sanctions that were the hardest to secure given the veto held by other permanent members of the Security Council. This new mechanism is not vulnerable to being blocked by any of the permanent members of the UNSC.

Most importantly, we can re-impose our own unilateral U.S. sanctions at any time in the future in response to a violation of the JCPOA. These are the sanctions that were the most powerful in driving Iran back to the negotiating table.

We have been able to count on our partners to enforce these sanctions in the past, and we have the tools to do so both unilaterally and multilaterally in the future should we need to.

Question:

Please explain to this Committee why the Administration feels obligated to allow for Iran to decide what measures are or are not sufficient in keeping the American people safe when Iran is the largest state sponsor of terrorism.

Answer:

No country dictates the national security of the United States. The Administration worked closely with Congress on the legislation to strengthen the Visa Waiver Program (VWP) and as a whole we believe the legislation both enhances the security of the homeland and allows for legitimate travel to the United States. Under the new law, the Secretary of Homeland Security may waive certain restrictions if he determines that such a waiver is in the law enforcement or national security interests of the United States. Recognizing Congressional concerns about blanket exemptions to the law, DHS and State worked closely together to identify groups of potential VWP travelers that could be considered for a waiver on a case-by-case basis. The Secretary of Homeland Security concurs with the judgement of the Secretary of State that it is in the national security interest of the United States to administer waivers for individual ESTA applicants in five designated categories of travelers; however, in no instance is travel under VWP guaranteed simply because an individual falls within one of these categories.

It should be noted that the P5+1 and European partners were essential in achieving the Joint Comprehensive Plan of Action (JCPOA) and cutting off Iran's pathways to a nuclear weapon, which is in the United States' national security interest. We have publicly defended the new law on visa waivers against charges that it violates our JCPOA commitments. But treating an otherwise eligible businessperson from a VWP partner country in Europe or elsewhere as a heightened security risk solely for engaging in business activities now permissible risks driving an unnecessary wedge between the United States and some of our closest partners at a time when we need to maintain a united front in this and other important diplomatic efforts.

We want to emphasize that each VWP traveler potentially eligible for a waiver will be carefully reviewed and waivers will only be administered on a case-by-case basis. As outlined, we believe there are significant national security interests for the United States to utilize this waiver authority without compromising the safety and security of the American people and the homeland.